OECD Public Governance Reviews

Promoting Integrity through the Reform of the Administrative Penalty System of Bulgaria

BUILDING A COMPREHENSIVE AND COHERENT LEGAL FRAMEWORK

This project was co-funded by the European Union via the Structural Reform Support Programme (REFORM/IM2020/017). This publication was produced with the financial assistance of the European Union. The views expressed herein can in no way be taken to reflect the official opinion of the European Union.

Please cite this publication as:
OECD (2022), *Promoting Integrity through the Reform of the Administrative Penalty System of Bulgaria: Building a Comprehensive and Coherent Legal Framework*, OECD Public Governance Reviews, OECD Publishing, Paris,
https://doi.org/10.1787/1be9905a-en.

ISBN 978-92-64-80609-2 (print)
ISBN 978-92-64-45553-5 (pdf)
ISBN 978-92-64-61975-3 (HTML)
ISBN 978-92-64-99941-1 (epub)

OECD Public Governance Reviews
ISSN 2219-0406 (print)
ISSN 2219-0414 (online)

Photo credits: Cover © RossHelen/Shutterstock.com, and Gearings image © OECD, designed by Christophe Brilhault.

Corrigenda to publications may be found on line at: www.oecd.org/about/publishing/corrigenda.htm.

Foreword

Administrative penalties are an important way to enforce compliance with legal instruments and regulations, and can apply to many areas of public administration, including procurement, environment, real estate, competition law, regulation of markets (energy, financial services, transport), and consumer protection. However, the entire process of enforcing laws and regulations through administrative penalties is subject to integrity risks, from ascertaining a violation, to imposing a sanction or deciding on appeals.

Corrupt behaviour on the part of those involved in the enforcement process can be encouraged or discouraged by various factors, including the extent to which the legal framework is clear, homogenous, comprehensive, coherent and objective. For example, if legal instruments have too narrow or too broad ranges of possible sanctions and no criteria for applying them, there is a greater possibility for officials to use the system for personal gain. In turn, such behaviour not only undermines the goals and objectives of regulations, but also broader compliance with the rules, citizens' trust in a country's public sector, rule of law, and investment climate.

Bulgaria has identified the prevention and sanctioning of corruption among the bodies in charge of enforcing the administrative legal framework as one of its anticorruption priorities. To address it, the Bulgarian government decided to undertake an in-depth analysis of the legislation on administrative penalties with a view to reforming it. This report – part of an EU-funded project under the Structural Reform Support Programme – seeks to support such efforts.

This report is part of OECD work on public integrity, which is the consistent alignment of, and adherence to, shared ethical values, principles and norms for upholding, and prioritising the public interest over private interests in the public sector. The OECD Recommendation on Public Integrity calls for countries to apply "fairness, objectivity and timeliness in the enforcement" through the disciplinary, administrative, civil, and/or criminal process.

The review was approved by the OECD Working Party of Senior Public Integrity Officials (SPIO) on 22 March 2022 and declassified by the Public Governance Committee on 28 April 2022 and prepared for publication by the Secretariat.

Acknowledgements

The report was prepared by the Directorate of Public Governance (GOV) under the leadership of Elsa Pilichowski, OECD Director for Public Governance and Julio Bacio Terracino, Head of the Public Sector Integrity Division in GOV. The report was co-ordinated by Giulio Nessi of the Public Sector Integrity Division with substantial input from Ralica Ilkova of Sofia University, Petya Mitreva of the University of National and World Economy and Oswald Jansen of the American University Washington College of Law. The report benefitted from the insights and comments from Alice Berggrun of the Public Sector Integrity Division and Elsa Gopala Krishnan of the Anti-corruption Division of the OECD. Editorial and administrative assistance was provided by Meral Gedik, Petra Burai, Viktoriya Minovska, Charles Victor and Aman Joal. The Bulgarian translation of the report was prepared by Ralica Ilkova and Petya Mitreva and edited by Viktoriya Minovska.

The report was carried out as part of the project “Overall reform of the administrative penalty proceedings” with funding by the European Union via the Structural Reform Support Programme and in co-operation with the European Commission's Directorate-General for Structural Reform Support (DG REFORM). The authors thank in particular Cristina Luchici and Vladimir Isaila of the European Commission's DG REFORM for their support and contributions to the report.

The OECD expresses its gratitude to the Government of Bulgaria as well as all the public institutions that took part in the process for their co operation, in particular the Council of Ministers of Republic of Bulgaria, the Ministry of Foreign Affairs; the Ministry of Interior; the Ministry of Energy; the Ministry of Health; the Ministry of Agriculture, Food and Forestry; the Ministry of Economy; the Ministry of Culture; the Ministry of Youth and Sports; the Ministry of Education and Science; the Ministry of Environment and Water; the Ministry of Defence; the Ministry of Justice; the Ministry of Regional Development and Public Works; the Ministry of Transport, Information Technology and Communications; the Ministry of Labour and Social Policy; the Ministry of Tourism; the Ministry of Finance; the State Agency for E-governance; the State Agency for Metrology and Technical Supervision; the National Revenue Agency; the Customs Agency; the State Financial Inspection Agency; the Bulgarian Food Safety Agency; the Executive Agency for Fisheries and Aquaculture; the Agency Road Infrastructure; the Executive Agency "General Labour Inspectorate"; the Agency for People with Disabilities; the Executive Agency "Road Traffic Administration"; the Executive Agency "Maritime Administration", the Executive Agency "Railway Administration"; the Executive Agency for Exploration and Maintenance of the Danube River; the Directorate General “Civil aviation administration”; the Consumer Protection Commission; the Financial Supervision Commission; Burgas Municipality; the Inspectorate of Sofia Municipality and the Regional Directorate of Forests – Lovech. Finally, Krasimir Bozhanov and Iskren Ivanov from the Council of Ministers' Modernisation of the Administration Department and, until May 2021, Petya Tyankova from the Office of the Deputy Prime Minister for Judicial Reform deserve special mention for co-ordinating all the activities, including the questionnaire answered by over 30 entities, the virtual fact-finding mission held between March and April 2021, and the virtual workshop organised in September 2021 where the preliminary recommendations were presented and discussed with representatives from public institutions and academia.

Table of contents

FIGURES

Follow OECD Publications on:

 *http://twitter.com/OECD_Pubs*

 *http://www.facebook.com/OECDPublications*

 *http://www.linkedin.com/groups/OECD-Publications-4645871*

 *http://www.youtube.com/oecdilibrary*

OECD Alerts *http://www.oecd.org/oecddirect/*

Executive summary

The reform of the administrative penalty legal framework forms part of Bulgaria's anti-corruption agenda. The Anti-corruption Strategy of Bulgaria 2015-2020 emphasised integrity risks in the enforcement of laws and regulations through administrative penalties and included the reform of the legal framework as part of the strategy to mitigate them. This approach was confirmed by the Anticorruption Strategy 2021-2027, which set as one of its priority objectives the improvement of legislation on the control and sanctioning of the administration with a view to limiting the scope for corrupt practices.

Although recent efforts and reforms have improved the legal framework, several challenges remain. The legal framework is fragmented and lacks coherence, creating risks of corrupt practices in its enforcement, and more generally endangering the rule of law and the capacity of the administration to carry out its functions effectively.

The report analyses key challenges of the legal framework on administrative penalties and proposes concrete and practical recommendations that will form the basis for developing proposals for legislative amendments. In particular, the report identifies three main areas where reform is most needed.

First, the scope of application of the legal framework could be more clearly and comprehensively defined. This is particularly true for the regime applicable to legal entities, whose liability arises when a natural person commits certain crimes and the legal entity has benefited or could benefit from it. Although the latest amendments to the Administrative Violations and Penalties Act (AVPA), which entered into force in December 2021 filled certain gaps, the liability of legal entities and sole traders could be regulated more comprehensively and in greater detail in relation to issues such as: the categories of crimes from which the legal entity may derive benefit; the status of persons whose criminal conduct can trigger liability; the criteria and incentives determining the penalty; and the incompatibilities for representing legal persons. Plus, there is no uniform practice in sanctioning branches of legal entities and entities without legal personality such as partnerships under civil law. Coherent and proportional rules could also be established for sanctioning the admitter and the principal when the offence is committed by their subordinates, since most special laws establish liability for admitters and, rarely, for managers who have ordered their subordinate employees to commit violations.

A second area where reform includes the typologies, criteria and levels of administrative penalties provided for in both the general and special legal framework. The introduction of new typologies of sanctions in the AVPA should be part of a broader strategy to increase compliance with penalties, considering that the collection rate of monetary fines is currently below 50%. Bulgaria recently introduced a new typology of sanction, unpaid work for the benefit of society; its implementation may reveal some gaps. In the meantime, additional typologies could be considered based on the experience of other EU member states, including the possibility to debar legal entities.

Ensuring the uniformity, coherency and proportionality of the level of sanctions through the special administrative legal framework is a significant challenge, for instance because the ranges of sanctions are eitehr too wide or too narrow. This could be addressed by intervening in all the special laws being affected by inappropriate levels of sanctions. Alternatively, or subsequently, Bulgaria could initiate a systemic reform by setting a limited number of sanction ranges and having each special law deciding the applicable one depending on the gravity of the offence.

Third, the reform of the legal framework should address several gaps and inconsistencies concerning procedural issues of administrative penal law. The AVPA contains very few provisions for investigating administrative violations, so it could either make more extensive reference to the relevant rules of the Code of Criminal Procedure or it could be integrated with a specific set of rules along with the rules proposed in the draft Code of Administrative Violations and Penalties of 2015.

From the perspective of those who enforce the legal framework, one of most significant challenges concerns difficulties in serving the acts and papers and thereby ensuring the participation of all actors in the proceedings, who in some cases take advantage of legal shortcomings to seek impunity. Additional rules for the AVPA are thus proposed for the serving of summonses and notices to natural and legal persons, including in cases when they are not residents of Bulgaria. It is also proposed to specify limited cases in which proceedings may take place *in absentia*, when even the offender has not been presented and served the act.

With regards to appeal proceedings, the reference to two different procedural regulations – criminal and administrative - is considered to cause contradictions and inconsistencies in practice. To address them, the AVPA could consider using only those regulations laid down in the Code of Criminal Procedure, given the origins and foundations of the Bulgarian administrative penal system. For the sake of procedural economy, the AVPA could regulate the consolidation, separation and suspension of proceedings. There is also a need to differentiate between preclusive time periods and statutes of limitations to allow more time to collect evidence, which some entities consider to be too short.

Another area of reform in the AVPA is the execution of penalties imposed abroad or the execution abroad of penalties imposed by Bulgarian administrative bodies. As pointed out by respondents to the OECD questionnaire and interviews, the issue of international legal co-operation in administrative penal cases is becoming more and more relevant, so the legal framework could explicitly and comprehensively regulate such cases. This could address situations when another EU member state or a third country has imposed an administrative penalty for a violation that is subject to sanction or has already been sanctioned by the Bulgarian law enforcement authorities. Similarly, a mechanism could be developed for collecting costs and pecuniary sanctions in administrative penal cases from foreigners without a permanent or known address the Republic of Bulgaria. To fully develop regulation involving foreigners and guarantee their procedural rights, more specific rules would also be needed for the translation and interpretation during proceedings.

1 The administrative penalty framework in Bulgaria

This chapter introduces the origins and development of administrative penalty law in Bulgaria and describes the applicable legal framework including its recent reforms. It addresses the relevance of ensuring the quality of administrative penalties for public sector integrity. The section also outlines the underlying goals of the analysis, the scope of the report as well as the challenges and ways of improvement for the regulations.

1.1. The relevance of administrative penalties for public sector integrity

Public entities are increasingly vested with the power to sanction illegal conducts which the legal system considers deserving punishment but not the consequences provided for by the criminal law system. As a consequence, besides compliance promotion activities, administrative penalties are commonly used by public entities to enforce legal instruments and regulations in nearly any area of public administration such as procurement, environment, real estate and city development, communications, competition, consumer protection, tax matters, financial markets, and road circulation. Such penalties have also grown following their provision in EU legal instruments, which envisage them in area such as competition law, regulation of markets (energy, financial services, transport), and consumer protection.

Failure to promote compliance, enforce regulatory requirements and impose administrative penalties, where needed, in a way that is fair, transparent and proportional to imposed risk, not only endangers/compromises/threatens the achievement of laws and regulations' goals, but it also has a severe impact on citizens' trust in public sector action and on the confidence in the investment climate and the rule of law. This is especially the case when the challenges in administrative enforcement are due to corrupt behaviour of control and sanctioning administrative authorities taking advantage of legal gaps and loopholes. Indeed, risks of corruption and ineffective enforcement can be higher when the legal framework is unclear, fragmented, incomplete or lacks objectivity, risk-responsiveness and proportionality.

The National Strategy for Prevention and Counteracting Corruption of Bulgaria of 2015-2020 (Anti-corruption Strategy 2015-2020) identified the prevention and sanctioning of corruption in the bodies in charge of enforcing the administrative legal framework as one of its priorities. In particular, the Anti-corruption Strategy noted that among the conditions favouring the emergence of corrupt behaviour within these bodies and throughout the related proceedings there are weaknesses in the legislation on administrative penalties. This was confirmed by the Anticorruption Strategy 2021-2027, which set as one of its priority objectives the improvement of the legislation on the control and sanctioning of the administration with a view to limiting the scope for corrupt practices. Although Bulgaria has put efforts and introduced reforms that have addressed some of the challenges of the legal framework in the last years, several issues remain.

1.2. The origins and development of administrative penalty law in Bulgaria

The Administrative Violations and Penalties Act ('AVPA')[1] is the key legal instrument governing administrative penalties and the application thereof in Bulgaria. The AVPA establishes the basic principles and foundations for the application of administrative penalties, while the types of administrative violations and penalties are established in more than three hundred sectorial laws that regulate different areas of public domain.

The AVPA was adopted in 1969, one year after the adoption of the Criminal Code, and the connection between the two legal instruments concerning basic concepts and legal foundations has been preserved ever since. Since 1989 it has been amended and supplemented more than 40 times and created a fragmented legal framework, whereas many of these amendments addressed specific problems that appeared at a particular moment and were not coherent with broader Bulgarian legislation. The weaknesses of the legal framework have been the subject of continuous academic and political debates aimed at improving the legal framework for the administrative penalties system. In recent years, several reforms have either been proposed or adopted and the most recent changes will enter into force on 23 December 2021 (Box 1.1).

Box 1.1. Recent reform of administrative penalty law in Bulgaria

In 2011, under the aegis of the Ministry of Justice, a Strategic document for continuing the reform of the administration of justice and the justice system in the field of administrative penalties for the period 2011-2014 was developed. This document outlined the legislative and organisational measures for prevention of and response to administrative violations. As part of these efforts, between 2012 and 2015 a working group established in the Ministry of Justice prepared a draft Code of Administrative Violations and Penalties which aimed at codifying the general rules applicable to administrative violations, administrative penalties and coercive administrative measures; the procedure for establishing the administrative violations, the procedure for imposing, appealing and application of administrative penalties and coercive measures; the guarantees for the protection of the rights and legitimate interests of citizens and their organisations. Eventually the draft code has not been submitted to the National Assembly for discussion.

In the period between 2016 and 2017, the former Centre for Prevention of and Counteraction to Corruption and Organized Crime prepared the report "Identification of existing corruption risks and practices in the supervisory and sanctioning activities of the administration. A proposed solution". This report identified the weaknesses related to the regulation and implementation of state policy in the administration's supervisory and sanctioning activities and proposed several measures to overcome them, which have also been considered in drafting the current report.

Most recently, with Decision no. 69 of 5 February 2018, the Council of Ministers of Bulgaria approved the Interdepartmental Working Group report on the topic of "Independence of the Judiciary and Corruption" which contained specific anti-corruption measures concerning the supervision and administrative penalty activities of the administration. In connection with the approved anti-corruption measures, a number of amendments to the AVPA have been approved by the National Assembly in December 2020 and the new amendments will enter into force on 23 December 2021.

1.3. Advancing the reform of the administrative penalty framework

Following request from Bulgaria and with the support of the European Commission under the Structural Reform Support Programme, starting from October 2020 the OECD has been providing technical support to the Government of Bulgaria in view of addressing existing challenges of the legal framework on administrative penalties and proposing legislative amendments in light of EU Member States' experience and good practices. As part of this project, the present report analyses the administrative penalty framework of Bulgaria and identifies key challenges and recommendations to address them. These recommendations will form the basis upon which the OECD will develop concrete proposals for Bulgaria's consideration.

In particular, the report addresses the issues emerged from an in-depth analysis of the AVPA and several special administrative laws in diverse sectors such as:

- Accounting Act;
- Act on the Operation of the Collective Investment Schemes and of Other Undertakings for Collective Investment;
- Bulgarian Identity Documents Act;
- Civil Aviation Act;
- Commercial Act;

- Commodity Exchanges and Markets Act;
- Consumer Protection Act;
- Credit Institutions Act;
- Customs Act;
- Cybersecurity Act;
- Decree for Combating Petty Hooliganism;
- Excises and Tax Warehouses Act
- Foreigners in the Republic of Bulgaria Act;
- Forest Act;
- Labour Code;
- Law on Excise Duties and Tax Warehouses;
- Law on the Protection of Classified Information;
- Payment Services and Payment Systems Act;
- Public Offering of Securities Act;
- Renewable Energy Act;
- Road Traffic Act;
- Road Transport Act;
- Roads Act;
- Tax-Insurance Proceedings Code;
- Tourism Act;
- Wine and Spirit Drinks Act.

The report also benefitted from the information collected through a questionnaire that was responded by around 30 public entities – including ministries, agencies as well as entities at the regional and municipal level – between December 2020 and March 2021 and during a virtual fact-finding mission involving several institutions held in March 2021. A workshop was also organised with key institutions in September 2021 to discuss the report findings and draft recommendations, and the report reflects the feedback shared by participants.

1.4. Scope of the report

The report is divided in three thematic areas related to the legal framework – subjective scope; typologies and levels of sanctions; procedural aspects – and provides recommendations as to how to address the identified challenges and enhance the fairness, effectiveness, objectivity, proportionality and responsiveness of its administrative penalty system, thereby mitigating the risks of corruption associated with its application. The report takes into consideration the OECD Toolkit and Best Practice Principles on Regulatory Enforcement and Inspections (OECD, 2014[1]; OECD, 2018[2]). It also introduces good practices from other EU Member States, in particular from six countries – Austria, Czech Republic, Germany, Lithuania, the Netherlands and Spain – which are expression of a mix of leading and diverse models developed in the European Union to sanction administrative violations and whose practices are – on a case-by-case basis - relevant and compatible for Bulgaria´s legal tradition and context.

The report focuses on the challenges and room for improvement of the legal framework, which a fundamental piece of the administrative penalty system. However, future work could address other key related areas of the system, in particular the institutional and governance ones. In Bulgaria, expertise in administrative penalty law exists within the institutions which are counterparts of the project – Office of the

Deputy Prime Minister for Judicial Reform (until May 2021) and Directorate for Modernization of Administration within the Council of Ministers – and the latter institution yearly collects some data on administrative penalties and proceedings as part of the Annual State of the Administration Report. The Anticorruption Strategy 2021-2027 has also planned the establishment and implementation of a single register of administrative and criminal proceedings, whose design and implementation will be the responsibility of different actors including the National Anti-corruption Council, the Administrative Reform Council, the State Agency for e-Government, the Chief Inspectorate of the Council of Ministers (Box 1.2).

Box 1.2. The objectives of the planned register for administrative penalty proceedings according to the Anti-corruption Strategy 2021-2027

The register of administrative penalty proceedings aims to address the problems of the administration's control and sanctioning activities related to: the lack of a uniform database of related proceedings; the lack of control over the performance of checks on compliance with administrative regimes; the lack of discretion as to the timeliness and uniform application of the law; the lack of complete and comprehensive information on the enforcement of the penalties imposed and the outcome of the enforcement of debts from fine; and the lack of a legal basis for the digitisation of administrative and criminal information and the exchange of information between administrative bodies.

The register will function as a single electronic database through an integrated information system that supports it, enabling the entry, processing, storage, and verification of recorded circumstances and aggregation of the results of the activities of the bodies entrusted with control and sanctioning powers.

The register will allow for timely reporting to the administration of expiry of procedural limits in view of better controlling the relevant activity of the administration, in particular over the bodies in charge of control and sanctioning powers.

Another objective of the register is to allow the structured storing and digitisation of the activities related to the issuing of final decisions of the sanctioning authority and the decisions establishing administrative infringements.

Source: (Government of Bulgaria, 2021[3])

Based on a preliminary research, European countries do not seem to assign a specific responsibility on administrative penalty policy as such to a single institution. At the same time, they ensure coherence of administrative penalties through their policy on legal and regulatory quality, which is usually the responsibility of center-of-government institutions or ministries of justice. For example, Austria, Germany, the Netherlands and Spain have developed technical guidance on the framing of legislation and in some cases specific guidelines concern the drafting of provisions creating administrative penalties, on enforceability and the choice between sanctioning systems (Box 1.3). Additional research and work could thus identify how Bulgaria could improve the governance of the administrative penalty system and define specific responsibilities on issues such as ensuring coherence of the relevant legal framework, providing guidance in preparing draft regulations providing for administrative penalties by single Ministries as well as centralising and using data on penalties and related proceedings.

Box 1.3. Ensuring quality of administrative penalty legislation in Austria, Germany, Spain and the Netherlands

The Federal Chancellery (Bundeskanzleramt) of Austria published a manual for legislative drafting (Handbuch der Rechtssetzungstechnik) and other legislative guidelines (Legistische Richtlinien). One of these guidelines involves the wording of provisions on obligations and prohibitions and their punishment. The Verfassungsdienst of the Bundeskanzleramt is entrusted with Legistik, the legislative technique and quality.

The Federal Ministry of Justice of Germany has published a Manual for Drafting Legislation (Handbuch der Rechtsförmlichkeit). Several instructions focus on Administrative Penalties (nr. 43, 59 and 81 of Appendix 2) of this Manual contains the 'Principles Regarding the Need for Sanctions in the Form of Administrative Fines, Especially in Relation to Measures of Administrative Compulsion' (available in English). Germany also developed a Manual on supplementary criminal provisions (Handbuch des Nebenstrafrechts, 2018) and the Guidance on Framing Criminal and Administrative Fines Provisions in Supplementary Criminal Provisions Outside of the Criminal Code. The Ministry of Justice also has a specific subdirectorate in charge – among other topics – of Germany's key administrative penalty law - the Regulatory Offences Act - under the Directorate General II dealing with Criminal law.

In Spain the Ministry of Presidency (Ministerio de la Presidencia) is entrusted by law with the task to ensure the co-ordination and quality of the State's normative activity. This entails the analysis of the technical quality of proposed legislation as well as the conformity of the proposed regulation with policies to limit administrative burdens and good regulation (Article 26, paragraph 9, Law 50/1997). For this purpose the Coordination and Normative Quality Office (Officina de Coordinación y Calidad normative) was created within the Ministry of Presidency. In 2005 the Spanish government set up guidelines to standardise approaches to law drafting (Directrices de técnica normativa). These guidelines do not contain models or guidelines on the drafting and co-ordination of offences and administrative penalties.

The Netherlands has created a Knowledge Center for Policy and Regulation (Kenniscentrum voor beleid en regelgeving) to support employees of central government entrusted with the development of policies and legislation. The prime minister has published Drafting instructions for legislation (Aanwijzingen voor de regelgeving). Legislative lawyers at central government are obliged to follow these instructions. The instructions also address issues such as the enforceability of regulations, the choice of methods of enforcement and between sanctioning systems. They also offer many models to frame specific provisions, such as provisions creating sanctioning powers. Next to this, on 14 April 2011 the Dutch government has issued other compulsory quality standards (*verplichte kwaliteitseisen*). One of these quality standards focuses on the principles determining the choice between sanctioning systems (Uitgangspunten bij de keuze van een sanctiestelsel).

Source: OECD Research; (Government of Germany, 2021[4])

References

Government of Bulgaria (2021), *National Strategy for Preventing and Countering Corruption in the Republic of Bulgaria (2021-2027)*, https://www.strategy.bg/StrategicDocuments/View.aspx?lang=bg-BG&Id=1353 (accessed on 8 October 2021). [3]

Government of Germany (2021), *Organisation plan of the Ministry of Justice and Consumer Protection*, https://www.bmjv.de/SharedDocs/Downloads/DE/Ministerium/Organisationsplan/Organisationsplan_EN.pdf?__blob=publicationFile&v=38 (accessed on 26 November 2021). [4]

OECD (2021), *Implementing the OECD Anti-Bribery Convention. Phase 4 Report: Bulgaria*, OECD, Paris, https://www.oecd.org/corruption/bulgaria-oecdanti-briberyconvention.htm (accessed on 27 October 2021). [5]

OECD (2018), *OECD Regulatory Enforcement and Inspections Toolkit*, OECD Publishing, Paris, https://dx.doi.org/10.1787/9789264303959-en. [2]

OECD (2014), *Regulatory Enforcement and Inspections*, OECD Best Practice Principles for Regulatory Policy, OECD Publishing, Paris, https://dx.doi.org/10.1787/9789264208117-en. [1]

Note

[1] This is referred to as 'Law on Administrative Offences and Sanctions' in (OECD, 2021[5]).

2 Persons liable for administrative penalties in Bulgaria

This chapter deals with the challenges emerged in relation to the categories of persons which can be liable for administrative violations. In particular, the analysis focuses on various aspects related to the administrative liability of legal persons - including specific typologies such as entities without legal personality, branches of legal entities and foreign legal entities. It also addresses the regime applicable to those who have oversight responsibilities over employees or subordinates as well as instigators, facilitators and admitters. While challenges in these areas exist in other OECD countries, a more comprehensive legal framework in Bulgaria in this area could help address the gaps and inconsistencies emerging from the analysis and the application.

2.1. Bulgaria could expand the liability of legal entities to branches of legal entities and entities without legal personality in the AVPA

The liability of legal entities and sole traders for non-fulfilment of an obligation to the state and the municipalities is regulated by art. 83 AVPA. In particular:

> *"A pecuniary sanction may be imposed on legal entities and sole traders for any failure to discharge their obligations to the state or the municipality stemming from and in connection with the performance of their activities in such cases as are provided for in a relevant law, by-law or decree of the Council of Ministers or ordinance of the municipal council."*

Through the latest amendments to the AVPA, which have entered into force on 23 December 2021, the rules governing the liability of legal entities and sole traders were supplemented by two new paragraphs laying down the rules on the liability in the event of legal succession of a legal person. According to the new provisions, in case of legal succession after the act establishing the administrative violation has been drawn up, the administrative penalty proceedings continue with the successor as its subject.

Although the latest amendments to the AVPA fill certain legal gaps as regards the liability of sole traders and legal entities, the question of the liability of branches of companies and the liability of entities without legal personality such as partnerships under civil law remains to be addressed.

With regards to branches of legal entities and sole traders, in some cases they are not registered as a separate legal entity and their functions are purely commercial. In such cases, the liability for failure to fulfil an obligation to the state or municipality lies with the company or the sole trader. This practice was also mentioned by the respondents in the course of interviews. However, in a number of situations, the branch of the legal entity or sole trader is a separate legal entity, which also raises the question of its financial liability for failure to comply with an administrative obligation. In this case the branch has its own legal status and property, so the legal liability does not arise for the parent legal entity but for the branch.

The absence of a legal framework for the liability of the branches of legal entities should be pointed out as a legislative gap, which leads to contradictions in the practice of administrative sanctioning authorities and courts. This legislative gap is also highlighted by the respondents to the OECD questionnaire. For example, it has been mentioned that branches of commercial companies and branches of foreign traders can be employers, but are not liable for administrative violations committed by them, as there are no applicable administrative penalty provisions in Article 412a of the Labour Code. This legislative gap is also established in other laws, but since it relates to the general question of persons subject to administrative penalty liability, this could be consistently addressed in the AVPA as proposed in Box 2.1. These proposed amendments would also allow providing clarity on the issue of legal representation of the branches of national and foreign legal entities, including the servicing the summons, notices and other documents addressed (cf. Box 4.10).

Box 2.1. Proposed Articles on liability of branches

Article 83, para 1a AVPA: "The provision of para 1 shall also be applied to the branches of the national and foreign legal entities, which have the status of trader according to art. 1 of the Commercial Act and any other civil organisation with economic activity."

Article 83, para 1b AVPA: "In case the branch of national or foreign legal entity does not have a status of a trader under art.1 of Commercial Act, the legal entity shall be held liable."

Source: OECD proposal

In spite of the general nature of article 4 of AVPA – which provides jurisdictional basis to commence administrative penalty proceedings, it would be appropriate to ensure that branches of both Bulgarian and foreign legal entities are explicitly included among the entities liable for administrative violations as done by Lithuania through Article 37 of the Lithuanian Law of Public Administration and in line with the definition of economic operator used in EU Law (Box 2.2).

Box 2.2. Scope of liability of legal persons in Lithuania

According to Article 37 of the Lithuanian Law on Public Administration, administrative penalties can be imposed on any "economic entity", which is a natural or legal person or any other organisation, a branch of the legal person or any other organisation which carries out economic activity. The relevant provisions read as follows:

"**Article 2** The basic concepts of this law:

(14) Economic entity - a natural or legal person or other organisation, a subdivision of a legal person or other organisation carrying out economic activities in the territory of the Republic of Lithuania, which is supervised by public administration entities."

The definition of economic operator in the Lithuanian Law on Public Administration allows for the liability of foreign legal entities as well as entities that have legal personality according to national law.

At EU level, according to settled case-law of the European Court of Justice, the concept of 'undertaking' covers any entity engaged in an economic activity, regardless of its legal status and the way in which it is financed, and any activity consisting in offering goods and services on a given market is an economic activity. In particular, the Court maintained that the term 'undertaking' should be understood as designating an economic unit even if in law that economic unit consists of several natural or legal persons, and that if such an economic entity infringes the competition rules, it is for that entity, consistently with the principle of personal liability, to answer for that infringement. Thus, the conduct of a subsidiary may be imputed to the parent company in particular where, although having a separate legal personality, that subsidiary does not decide independently upon its own conduct on the market, but carries out, in all material aspects, the instructions given to it by the parent company, having regard in particular to economic, organisational and legal links between those two legal entities. That is the case because, in such a situation, the parent company and its subsidiary form a single economic unit and therefore form a single undertaking. Thus, the fact that a parent company and its subsidiary constitute a single undertaking enables the European Commission to address a decision imposing fines to the parent company, without having to establish the personal involvement of the latter in the infringement.

Source: OECD research; (OECD, 2016[1]); Judgment of the Court of First Instance (Second Chamber) of 12 December 2006. SELEX Sistemi Integrati SpA v Commission of the European Communities, https://eur-lex.europa.eu/legal-content/GA/TXT/?uri=CELEX:62004TJ0155.

The lack of legislation as regards the liability of entities without legal personality such the one provided for by art. 357 of the Law on Obligations and Contracts should be pointed out as a gap in the legislation on administrative penalties, as also highlighted in the course of the fact finding interviews.

According to art. 357, para. 1 of the Law on Obligations and Contracts, 'under the contract of partnership two or more persons agree to unite their activities for achieving a common business objective.' The partnership is not a legal entity; it is subject to civil law or civil liability for failure to fulfil an obligation arising from a contract with another individual, but it is not liable for failure to fulfil obligations towards the state or municipalities.

A major challenge to the legal framework is that the entities such as those under art. 357 of the Law on Obligations and Contracts do not own any property. According to art. 359, para. 1 of the Law on Obligations and Contracts, 'Everything acquired by the partnership is jointly owned by the partners'. Art. 359, para. 2 stipulates that, unless otherwise agreed, the shareholders' shares are equal.

Another entity without legal personality is the consortium referred to in art. 275 of the Commercial Act. According to the definition in art. 275 of the Commercial Act, a consortium is a contractual association of traders who carry out a certain activity. On the basis of art. 276 of the Commercial Act, the substance of this legal form can be implemented in two ways - as partnership under civil law or as a commercial company. In the first case, the consortium is a partnership (to which the provisions of art. 357 to 364 of the Law on Obligations and Contracts apply) and is not a legal entity, and in the second, the consortium takes the form of a commercial company in one of its five types permitted under the Bulgarian law.

Insofar as it is possible that the activities of a partnership under civil law also lead a failure to fulfil an obligation towards the state or a municipality, the possibility of assigning them a status of legal entities for the purposes of administrative penalties could be considered. Hence, where an entity without legal personality has failed to fulfil an obligation to the state or the municipality, its liability is objective and its status for the purposes of administrative penalties should be considered the same as that of legal entities. In order to introduce the liability of such entities Article 83 of the AVPA could amended as proposed in Box 2.3.

Box 2.3. Proposed Article 83(5)

"**Article 83, para. 5.** The provisions of paragraphs 1 and 2 shall also apply to:

1. Companies under the Law on Obligations and Contracts and consortia of commercial companies, when they are not commercial companies, where there has been a breach of obligation towards the state or the municipality in the course of their activities, unless otherwise stipulated by a special law;

2. Persons under subparagraphs 1, registered in another state, performing activities in the Republic of Bulgaria through a branch, unless otherwise stipulated by a special law."

Note: This proposal was discussed in the working group responsible for the latest amendments of the AVPA, but eventually was not adopted.

2.2. Bulgaria could provide for a more comprehensive liability regime for legal entities that enriched themselves or would enrich themselves from a crime

Bulgarian law provided for the liability of legal entities that have enriched themselves or would enrich themselves from a crime committed, for the first time in 2005 with the entry into force of the Law on Amendments of the AVPA, promulgated, SG 79 of 4 October 2005, which established the provisions of Art. 83a-83e of the law. In 2015 and 2020, the institute was seriously reformed. However, not all weaknesses in the legal framework have been dealt with, and the ongoing application of the institute by the courts is likely to reveal additional weaknesses not yet established by legal theory.

The liability of legal persons under Chapter 4 of the AVPA arises from a crime committed by a natural and criminally responsible person, from which those legal entities have benefited or could benefit. This gives rise to two types of legal liability: criminal liability for the natural person who has committed the crime and administrative liability for the legal person who has benefited or could benefit. In other words, the liability of the legal person is not criminal but pecuniary, which is in line with the legal provisions adopted by other EU countries such as Germany and Italy.

In the first ten years of the introduction of the pecuniary liability of legal persons for a criminal offence in Bulgaria the concept has not delivered the expected results. The most significant problem for the realisation of the liability of these legal entities was the linking of the proceedings under Article 83a of the AVPA to the criminal proceedings against the responsible natural person. Therefore, in 2015 the institute was seriously revised. Both the substantive rules governing the liability of legal persons who have benefitted or would benefit by the commission of a criminal offence and the proceedings for the realisation of their liability have evolved and this has led to a sharp increase in the number of cases, which in turn revealed gaps and weaknesses in the regulation, which were not addressed by the 2015 reform.

This created the need for another legislative initiative to supplement and improve the institute's rules, which was carried out by the Law Amending and Supplementing the AVPA, promulgated in State Gazette No 109 of 22 December 2020. However, they have not address all the existing challenges and legal gaps which are illustrated in the following paragraphs. Additional areas of improvement with regards to the scope of corporate liability for foreign bribery and related offences have also been identified by the OECD Working Group on Bribery in its Phase 4 Report.[1]

2.2.1. Bulgaria could regulate the liability of the legal entities in greater detail

Currently the liability of the legal entities under Art. 83a and the following of AVPA arises in case of a crime has been committed by natural persons from which legal entities have profited or could have profited. The subjects of crime are exhaustively listed in art. 83a, para 1, items 1-4 of the AVPA. However, the liability of legal entities under the Bulgarian law is not criminal. It is probably due to these considerations that the institute was systematically regulated by the AVPA. However, the current legal framework does not allow for a detailed regulation of several specific aspects related to the liability of legal entities. In order to address them more comprehensively, Bulgaria could either amend Chapter IV of the AVPA on "Administrative punitive sanctions to legal persons and sole entrepreneurs" or regulate the liability of legal entities in a separate legislative instrument. While the stand-alone statutes on liability of legal persons are not common in the EU, Bulgaria could consider the examples of Italy and Slovenia if it decides to opt for the latter option. (Italy, 2001[2]); (Slovenia, 2005[3])

2.2.2. The catalogue of crimes determining the liability of legal entities could be expanded

Under the current regulation, not every crime provided for in the Special Part of the Penal Code determinates the liability of legal entities. Such are only those listed in Art. 83a, para. 1 of AVPA - fraud, extortion, human trafficking, money laundering, etc. Among these crimes are all crimes against EU funds.

However, the range of crimes that determine the liability of legal entities is considered to be incomplete. Thus, in the catalogue of crimes under Art. 83a, para. 1 of AVPA there are crimes from which legal entities could not possibly derive any benefit, even in theory (for example, rape under Article 152 of the Penal Code); at the same time, other crimes that could lead to illegal benefits for legal entities (e.g. certain crimes related to documents), are not listed. In regulating the range of offences leading to liability for the benefiting legal entity Bulgaria could consider two models:

1. A comprehensive and detailed list of crimes whose catalogue can be expanded, as done in Italy; (Italy, 2001[2]) or
2. Liability of the legal entity in each case of a crime committed as done in Slovenia. (Slovenia, 2005[3]).

2.2.3. The range of persons whose criminal activity leads to the liability of legal entities could be clarified to cover cases where they assist or attempt the commission of a crime

According to art. 83a, para 1 of AVPA, the possible subjects of the crime from which the liability of the legal entities is derived, are four categories of natural persons: 1. a person empowered to determine the will of the legal person; 2. a person who represents the legal person; 3. a person elected as a controlling or a supervising body of the legal person; 4. a worker or employee to whom the legal person has assigned certain duties, whereby the crime has been committed in the process of performing this work or in connection with it. These categories of persons could be held criminally liable under the Bulgarian Penal Code, as otherwise the Bulgarian law enforcement authorities would not be empowered to hold the legal entity liable. It means that if the person committed the crime is not legally responsible under the Criminal Code, the Bulgarian court could not decide if the act is a crime, including in the context of the institute of art. 83a of AVPA.

There is no obstacle to engaging the responsibility of the corporation when the persons from the first three categories are only facilitators or instigators in the commission of the crime from which the legal entity has benefited. However, if the person referred to in Art. 83a, para 1, item 4 is only an instigator, liability of the legal entity does not arise pursuant to Article 83(a)(3). Such difference is difficult to explain so the legislator could consider extending the scope of the institute to all categories of persons listed in Article 83(a)(1). Indeed, it is quite possible that they can all be instigators or facilitators in committing the crime to the benefit of the legal entity – employer.

2.2.4. Bulgaria could introduce additional and more precise criteria for the individualisation of administrative penalties for legal entities as well as incentives to assist enforcement agencies

The principle of individualisation of the penalty is laid down in Article 27 para. 2 of AVPA:

> *Art. 27. (1) The administrative penalty shall be determined according to the provisions of this Act within the limits of the penalty provided for the committed violation.*
>
> *(2) Taken into consideration in determining the penalty shall be the burden of the offence, the motives for its commitment and other attenuating and aggravating circumstances, as well as the proprietary status of the offender.*
>
> *(3) The attenuating circumstances shall substantiate the imposition of a lenient penalty and the aggravating - of a more serious sanction.*
>
> *(4) The replacement of the penalties stipulated for the violations by a more lenient in kind shall not be admitted except in the cases stipulated by art. 15, para 2.*
>
> *(5) (Suppl. – SG, 109/20, in force from 23.12.2021) Not admitted shall also be determining of penalties under the stipulated lowest size of the sanctions of pecuniary sanction and temporary deprivation of right to practice a definite profession or activity, apart from the cases, provided by the law.*

These principles are an expression of the traditional concept that the penalty, as an appropriate measure of liability, must be proportionate to the seriousness of the offence committed and the offender's personality have to be taken into account. However, the individualisation of the liability of the entities referred to in Article 83 AVPA should follow different rules on individualisation. These may be the seriousness of the failure to comply with the obligation towards the state or municipalities, including the length of the period in which a breach occurred, the harmful effects of the failure to comply, the financial situation of the legal entity and the sole trader, facts and circumstances relating to the previous sanctioning of the entity, etc.

A good basis for formulating a legislative proposal is the provision of Article 83a para. 5 AVPA (order, SG No 109/22.12.2020, in force since 23.12.2021), which will support Bulgarian courts in determining the amount of sanctions against a legal person. According to such provision:

> *In determining the amount of the pecuniary sanction, the gravity of the committed crime, the financial condition of the legal person, the assistance for detection of the crime and for compensation of the damages from the crime, the amount of the benefit and other circumstances shall be taken into account.*

This reform provided for specific rules to individualise the responsibility of legal entities that have enriched themselves or would enrich themselves from a crime. However, the liability of legal persons should be individualised only where the advantage — actually obtained or possible — is of a pecuniary nature and is lower than the special maximum of the penalty of BGN 1 000 000; where the advantage is not of a material nature, and where the value of the financial advantage cannot be established. On the other hand, the penalty should not be individualised when the pecuniary advantage is BGN 1 000 000 or more, as in these cases art. 83A, para. 1 of the AVPA does not allow for the discretion of the court — the legal person should be subject to a financial penalty up to the maximum amount provided for by the law.

Another important point is that only the pecuniary penalty is to be individualised, and not the other cumulative penalty imposed on legal persons — the confiscation of the advantage in favour of the state. The latter only corresponds to the size of the advantage and does not take other circumstances into account.

In spite of the progress in individualising the administrative penalties for legal entities, Bulgaria is still lacking a 'responsive enforcement approach' according to which, enforcement actions should be differentiated depending on the profile and behavior of legal entities to promote compliance more effectively. Bulgaria could consider the guidance provided by the Council of Europe to further improve the determination of the amount of sanctions against legal persons (Box 2.4). in view of including consideration of issues such as the duration of the breach, the degree of responsibility of the legal person, specific indicators to measure the financial condition of the legal person, the losses to the third parties and previous breaches of the legal persons.

Box 2.4. Toolkit and guidance of the Council of Europe on individualisation of penalties for legal persons based on the Fourth EU Anti-Money Laundering Directive

When determining the type and level of sanctions or measures, the competent authorities shall take into account all relevant circumstances, including where applicable:

- the gravity and the duration of the breach;
- the degree of responsibility of the legal person held responsible;
- the financial strength of the legal person held responsible, as indicated by, for example, the total turnover of the legal person held responsible;
- the benefit derived from the breach by the legal person held responsible, insofar as it can be determined;
- the losses to third parties caused by the breach, insofar as they can be determined;
- previous breaches by the natural or legal person held responsible.

Source: (Council of Europe, 2020[4]).

Although Article 83a paragraph 5 now includes assistance for detection of the crime as one of the criteria to individualise penalties, additional provisions could be introduced to incentivise legal persons to assist enforcement agencies as done in other EU countries which included co-operation as one of the mitigating factors in determining the degree of the penalty (Box 2.5).

Box 2.5. Incentive mechanisms for legal entities in Slovenia and Spain

The law in Slovenia provides for certain mechanisms to encourage legal persons to assist law enforcement authorities. Thus, if, following the commission of the offense, a management or supervisory body voluntarily turns in the offender, a reduced penalty may be imposed on the legal person. If, after the commission of the offence, the management or supervisory body of a legal person voluntarily and immediately orders the recovery of an unlawfully obtained property or provides compensation for the damage caused by the offense or reports information as regards the liability of other legal persons, the legal person may not be punished.

According to the Slovenian legislation, the court may impose a conditional sentence on a legal person instead of a pecuniary sanction. In case of a conditional conviction, the court may set a pecuniary sanction of up to EUR 500 000 and at the same time order that the sentence not be enforced if the legal person does not commit a new offense for a period set by the court, which may not be shorter than one year and longer than five years (probation period).

Similarly, in Spain legal entities can try to mitigate sentence by "confess[ing] the offence to the authorities, before knowing that there is a criminal procedure" against it and by "collaborat[ing] in the investigation ... at any time within the proceedings" by "producing ... new evidence".

Source: (OECD, 2016[11])

2.2.5. The legal framework could introduce separate sanctions when a legal entity has benefited from two or more crimes

It is quite possible for the legal entity to have benefited from two or more crimes committed by one or more natural persons among those specified in Art. 83a, para. 1 of the AVPA. At the legislative level, however, the question of whether in these cases a single sanction or a separate sanction for each of the crimes is imposed, has not been resolved. Bulgaria could thus consider introducing rules according to which for every violation the legal entity is subject to a separate sanction, which is also served separately. This approach is established for the individuals responsible under the Penal Code. In case of multiple crimes before a sentence has been enacted for any of them, the court, upon determining the penalty for each crime individually, shall impose the most severe of them. In this way, the principle of "absorption" of punishments was introduced. This principle is also applicable if a convicted person is sentenced with two or more different sentences, he will have to endure the most severe of them.

2.2.6. The regulation of the statute of limitations for legal entities could align with the regime applicable to natural persons

A significant weakness of the regulation of the liability of legal entities for a crime under the AVPA since the establishment of the institute fifteen years ago has been the lack of explicit regulation of the legal facts, the occurrence of which leads to extinction of the liability of legal entities that have enriched themselves or would enrich themselves from a crime.

The legal gap in this regard has led to an extremely contradictory practice in the application of the law. Thus, in some judicial acts it was accepted that the statute of limitations is inapplicable to legal entities, precisely because of the lack of legal regulation, in others - that the liability of legal entities is extinguished with the expiration of the terms equal in duration to those established for the criminally responsible natural persons, and in third - that the limitation periods established for repayment of the liability of the legal entities for administrative violations shall apply.

With the reform of the administrative penalty framework in 2020, the established legal gap was partly addressed with the introduction of a new para. 8 in Art. 83a of the AVPA. According to this para. 8, the administrative liability of the legal entity shall be repaid upon expiration of a term equal in duration to that under Art. 81, para. 3 of the Penal Code, as of the date of commission of the crime from which the legal entity has enriched itself or would enrich itself.

To further complement the existing gaps, Bulgaria could consider adopting the model established for natural persons to calculate the limitation periods, the expiry of which extinguishes the liability of legal persons. The length of those periods should correspond to the penalty provided for the offense committed and not to the limitation periods for the offenses punishable by pecuniary sanction. This will avoid the possibility of contradictory interpretation on the question of how the length of the limitation period is calculated, the expiration of which extinguishes the possibility to engage the liability of the legal entity that has enriched itself or would enrich itself from a crime - whether in view of the rules under Art. 81, para. 3, supra art. 80, para. 1, items 1–5 of the Penal Code, depending on the punishment provided for the committed crime, or in view of the rule under Art. 81, para. 3, supra art. 80, para. 1, item 5 of the Penal Code, which regulates the limitation period for crimes punishable by a pecuniary sanction.

2.2.7. Bulgaria could provide for detailed rules on the appointment and incompatibility of legal entities' representatives

Although the proceedings before the courts for imposing a pecuniary sanction on legal entities that have enriched themselves or would enrich themselves from a committed crime was deeply reformed in both 2015 and 2020, its regulation remains insufficient in relation to the procedural representation of legal entities before the court, for example when the guilty natural person is a legal representative of a legal entity.

Currently, the legal provisions of the Criminal Procedure Code are applicable, although these rules are intended to regulate the procedural legal relationship between the court and the defendant - a natural person. In this context, Bulgaria could consider introducing some specific rules on appointing or incompatibilities of legal persons' representatives along the example provided by the legal framework of Slovenia and Romania (Box 2.6).

Box 2.6. Rules on representation of legal persons in Slovenia and Romania

The Slovenian Law of Liability of Legal Persons for Criminal Offences Act 2005 regulates the representation of legal persons in articles 31 – 32. They include the prohibition for the accused legal person to be legally represented by someone called as a witness in the same matter or by the person against whom proceedings are being brought because of the same criminal offence, except if this is the only member of the accused legal person.

According to Romanian law, the legal person is called upon to participate in the proceedings. It is represented by its legal representative; if criminal proceedings are initiated against the legal representative of the legal person for the same or related offenses, the legal representative designates a representative; in the latter case, if the legal person has not appointed a proxy, a certified proxy is appointed by the public prosecutor or by the court. The participation of the prosecutor in these cases is mandatory.

Source: OECD Research; (Slovenia, 2005[3])

Although the proceedings before the courts for imposing a property sanction on legal entities that have enriched themselves or would enrich themselves from a committed crime have been seriously reformed in both 2015 and 2020, its regulation remains extremely concise.

2.3. The AVPA could ensure coherency in the special legislation concerning the liability regime of admitters and managers who ordered the commission of an administrative violation

The general norm which provides for administrative penalty liability of the managers is Article 24, para. 2 of the AVPA:

> *Liable for administrative violations committed in carrying out the activity of enterprises, establishments and organisations shall be the workers and employees who have committed them, as well as the chiefs who have ordered or admitted their commitment."*

In accordance with art.10 of the AVPA, the liability of so-called 'admitters' - those who have not prevented the commission of administrative offences by their subordinates - is envisaged as an administrative violation in a number of special administrative laws.

> *In cases of administrative violations instigators, facilitators and concealers, as well as those who have admitted them shall be punished only in the cases stipulated by the respective law or decree.*

Under the Bulgarian legal system, the institution of complicity includes incitement, assistance and commission. In criminal law, accomplices are always punished by the penalty provided for in respect of the offense committed, and their liability is ancillary, that is, it only arises if the offender commits the offence for which he is instigated or assisted. Administrative penalty law establishes the opposite principle and provides for administrative liability for complicity only in the cases provided for by the special laws. This legislative solution deserves support as not all administrative laws regulate public relations which can be damaged in the course of activity of undertakings, establishments and organisations — where admission is possible. However, in the various legislative acts, the grounds for the liability of the principal and the admitter are different. In some laws, the principal and the admitter are legally liable only where an employee has committed an administrative offence. In other cases, the liability of the principal and the admitter arises together with the liability as manager of a legal person if, as such, the perpetrator has admitted that the legal person does not to fulfil its obligations under art. 83 of the AVPA to the state or the municipality. The best approach is to establish liability for an admitter or the person who orders the violation or failure to fulfil an obligation as established, for example, in Article 96, para. 5, subparagraph 1, letters (b) — (d) of the Road Transport Act:

> *He who commits the following shall be punished by a pecuniary sanction or a financial penalty of BGN 1000:*
>
> *1. (amended, — SG No 9/2017) which:*
>
> ....
>
> *(b) allows or orders for the public transport or transport at their own expense of passengers or goods by means of a vehicle which is not technically fit for purpose;*
>
> *(c) allows or orders for the public transport or transport at their own expense of passengers or goods by means of a vehicle which has not been subjected to a pre-road technical inspection;*
>
> *(d) (new — SG Issue No. 60/2020, in force as of 07.07.2020) allows or orders transportation by a motor vehicle the driver of which is not provided with a certified copy of a Community licence.*

Another such example is Article 143, para. 1, subparagraph 9 of the Civil Aviation Act: 'The following shall be liable to a pecuniary sanction of BGN 3 000 to BGN 10 000: he who performs, orders or permits a flight with an aircraft in conditions not compatible with its exploitation features;'.

The analysis of the special administrative legislation shows that these examples are rather exceptional. Most administrative laws establish liability for admitters and, quite rarely, for managers who have ordered their subordinate employees to commit violations. Thus, the special administrative legislation treats the inaction of executives who have not prevented their subordinates from committing violations more severely than the actions of the same executives where they have ordered the commission of administrative offenses. This demonstrates the lack of a uniform approach to persons subject to administrative penalty liability and leads to gaps and inconsistencies in the legal framework.

For example, the Cybersecurity Act, art. 120, para. 1 and 2, liability is provided for the perpetrator and the admitter, but not for the person who ordered the violation:

> *(1) Anyone who commits an offence under Article 31 shall be liable to a pecuniary sanction of BGN 100 to 500.*
>
> *(2) The penalty referred to in paragraph 1 shall also be imposed on the head of an organisational entity or of an information security officer who commits an offence under Article 31.'*
>
> *It is, however, quite logical that the head of the organisational unit not only admitted, but also ordered the commission of the violation.*

Another weakness is that the extent of the admitter's liability has been resolved differently. In some laws there is no differentiation between the penalties for admission and commission. For example, art. 130, para. 1 of the Law on the Protection of Classified Information stipulates that a person who commits or admits an infringement under art. 108, para. 3 of the same Act is punishable by a pecuniary sanction of BGN 500 to 2 000 if the act does not constitute a criminal offence. In this and a number of other laws, the liability of the admitter and the liability of the perpetrator are differentiated, with the liability of the admitted being more or less severe than that of the perpetrator. For example, art. 124, para. 1 of the Law on the Protection of Classified Information stipulates that 'Any person who commits an offence under art. 86 shall be liable to a pecuniary sanction of BGN 3 000 to 10 000' and paragraph 3 provides for a pecuniary sanction between BGN 300 and BGN 2 000 for admission. This inconsistent approach to the liability of the admitter (as well as that of the principal) is also observed in other legal acts such as the Road Traffic Act.

It would therefore be appropriate to find a solution to that question in the general administrative law which should stipulate, in the cases provided for by the special legislation, that the admitter and the principal be punished by the same penalty as provided for the offence committed by their subordinates. The same approach applies to the criminal liability of the admitter for a crime under art. 285 of the Penal Code, whereas the admitter is punished by the same penalty provided for the crime committed, and has been adopted by other EU countries (Box 2.7).

Box 2.7. Aiding and abetting in Austria, Czech Republic and Germany

In Austria, according to Article 7 of VStG who deliberately causes another person to commit an administrative offence or who deliberately facilitates an administrative offence committed by another person is subject to the punishment determined for such offence even in case the actual offender is not liable to punishment.

In the Czech Republic, pursuant to Section 13 (4) of Act No. 250/2016 Coll., where a law so provides, the offender is also a natural person who deliberately causes in another person decision to commit an offence (abettor) or makes possible or easier committing offense by another person (aider) if it is a finished offense or an attempt to commit it, if an attempt is sanctioned.

In Germany the concept of "perpetrator" is unified, with no distinction between other forms of participation (e.g. co-perpetrator, instigator, accessory). Each participant is deemed to have committed a regulatory offence regardless of how he/she contributed to fulfilling the factual elements of the offence (section 14 OWiG).

Source: (European Committee on Crime Problems, 2020[5]).

Another option is the use of a legislative technique when describing the composition of offenses for perpetrators, principals and admitters: 'whoever orders, admits or commits...' Such technique is used by a number of laws, for example, the already mentioned provision of art. 130, para. 1 of the Law on the Protection of Classified Information or Art. 143, para. 1, item 9 of the Civil Aviation Act, which provides for a pecuniary sanction of BGN 3 000 to 10 000, for a person who: perform, order or admit a flight to be performed in a technically defective aircraft; an aircraft to be flown in conditions that do not comply with its performance.

The same approach could be applied not only in order to establish the administrative liability of the admitters, but also with regard to authorising officers, in cases where the operating rules imply a hierarchical relationship between employees on the one hand and senior officials on the other.

References

Council of Europe (2020), *Liability of Legal Persons for Corruption Offences*, https://rm.coe.int/liability-of-legal-persons/16809ef7a0 (accessed on 25 June 2021). [4]

European Committee on Crime Problems (2020), *Replies to Questionnaire on Administrative Sanctions*, https://rm.coe.int/cdpc-2019-1-replies-to-questionnaire-on-administrative-sanctions/168093669b (accessed on 24 June 2021). [5]

Italy (2001), *Legislative Decree 231 of 2001*, https://sherloc.unodc.org/cld/uploads/res/document/legislative-decree-8-6-2001-n-231_html/Legislative_Decree_8-6-2001_n_231_EN.pdf (accessed on 24 June 2021). [2]

OECD (2021), *Implementing the OECD Anti-Bribery Convention. Phase 4 Report: Bulgaria*, OECD, Paris, https://www.oecd.org/corruption/bulgaria-oecdanti-briberyconvention.htm (accessed on 27 October 2021). [6]

OECD (2016), *The Liability of Legal Persons for Foreign Bribery: A Stocktaking Report*, OECD, Paris, https://www.oecd.org/daf/anti-bribery/Liability-Legal-Persons-Foreign-Bribery-Stocktaking.pdf (accessed on 24 June 2021). [1]

Slovenia (2005), *Liability of Legal Persons for Criminal Offences Act*, https://sherloc.unodc.org/cld/uploads/res/document/svn/liability-of-legal-persons-for-criminal-offences-act_html/Slovenia_Liability_of_Legal_Persons_for_Criminal_Offences_Act.pdf (accessed on 24 June 2021). [3]

Note

[1] According to the OECD Working Group on Bribery, the legal framework does not provide for an effective jurisdictional base to commence proceedings against legal persons, including where the legal person uses non-nationals to bribe on its behalf abroad; unduly restricts proceedings to cases where the natural person perpetrator is prosecuted or convicted; and poses serious impediments to the effective sanctioning of legal persons for foreign bribery. (OECD, 2021[6])

3 Typologies, criteria and levels of penalties in Bulgaria

This chapter addresses the challenges of the legal framework of Bulgaria in ensuring that the typologies, criteria and levels of administrative penalties imposed when necessary, are capable to provide a proportional and coherent response to administrative breaches. For this purpose, it considers the general rules laid down in the AVPA but also a sample of special laws exemplifying the various typologies of problems related to the level of penalties. In this context, the report makes specific recommendations to create more differentiated administrative penalties to maximize compliance, but also starts a debate to reform the system of penalties as a whole. The report also analyses other related issues such as the relationship between similar administrative offences and crimes, as well as the regime for repeated and systemic violations.

3.1. Bulgaria could expand the typologies of penalties to increase their effectiveness and deterrence

Currently, the sanction system of the AVPA includes three main types of penalties: public reprobation, fine and temporary deprivation of right to practice a certain profession or activity. The fine is the main penalty provided for in the law and used in practice. (Figure 3.1) As an imposed punishment it is an amount of money determined by the law which does not depend on the income of the offender, hence often remains unpaid due to lack of income or property of the offender. Public reprobation is practically an inapplicable and ineffective punishment. Special administrative legislation contains administrative penalty provisions that establish relatively up-to-date systems of protective measures — sanctions and corrective administrative measures. These include the Protection of public order during sports events act and the Road Traffic Act.

Figure 3.1. Number of administrative penalties imposed in 2019 by typology of penalty

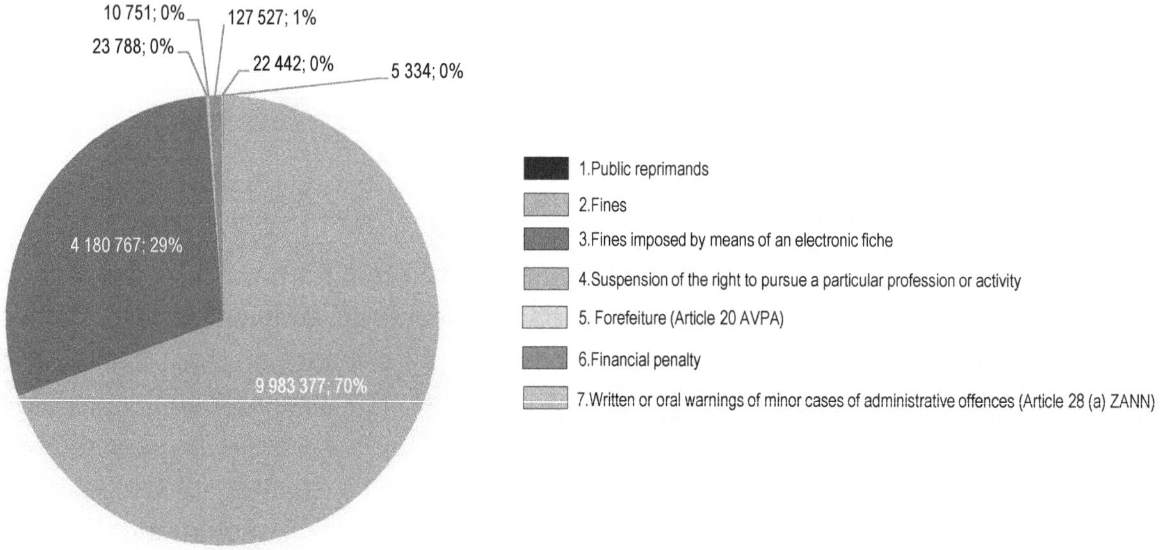

10 751; 0%
127 527; 1%
23 788; 0%
22 442; 0%
5 334; 0%
4 180 767; 29%
9 983 377; 70%

1.Public reprimands
2.Fines
3.Fines imposed by means of an electronic fiche
4.Suspension of the right to pursue a particular profession or activity
5. Forefeiture (Article 20 AVPA)
6.Financial penalty
7.Written or oral warnings of minor cases of administrative offences (Article 28 (a) ZANN)

Source: 2019 Annual State of the Administration Report.

The system of penalties has remained unchanged until 2020 despite the changing social and economic conditions in the country as well as the discussion around this topic. In 2017 the report of the Centre for the Prevention and Combating of Corruption and Organised Crime (CPCCOC) on 'Identification of existing corruption risks and practices in carrying out the control and sanctioning activities of the administration. A solution model', concluded that offenders have a widespread sense of impunity as a direct and immediate consequence of the State's inability to recover pecuniary sanctions/administrative punitive sanctions imposed with penal decrees. The above is evidenced by the response to the CPCCOC by the Executive Forestry Agency (EFA), which states that the average annual collection rate of the pecuniary sanctions and administrative punitive sanctions imposed is around 13-16%, but the main problem identified by the EFA is precisely the feeling of impunity of offenders, leading to further violations. The same challenges has emerged from the Annual State of the Administration Report of 2019 (Figure 3.2) as well as in the answers to the OECD questionnaire and interviews.

Figure 3.2. Percentage of fines and other pecuniary sanctions collected in 2019

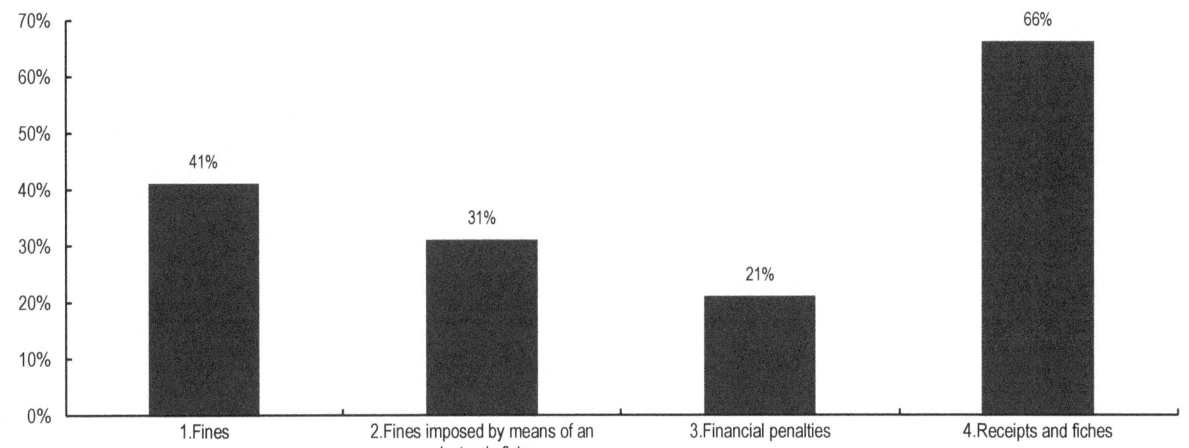

Source: 2019 Annual State of the Administration Report.

The report from the CPCCOC highlighted the need to introduce new, alternative measures of control and impact on offenders, beyond the already established types of pecuniary sanctions. These measures to be imposed separately or cumulatively with other sanctions, in analogy with probation in sanction system of criminal law. For example, replacement of the pecuniary sanction with another sanction could be possible in case of non-compliance without good reason. The report also pointed out that the normative establishment of a variety of alternative administrative measures will lead to the achievement of the goals of general and individual prevention and, in general, increase of the collection rate of the financial penalties is expected. In this way, the rehabilitation/reform effect of the punishment will be achieved.

The new law amending the AVPA in 2020 included a new punishment – unpaid work for the benefit of society. However, it does not overcome the gap identified by the CPCCOC because this new punishment is not an alternative to the other administrative penalties, especially alternative to the fine. According to the new provision of Art.13, para 2 of AVPA, for an administrative violation, committed repeatedly or on a systematic basis, a penalty of unpaid work for the benefit of society may be provided, which shall be imposed independently or simultaneously with the punishments under Para.1 (public reprobation, fine and temporary deprivation of right to practice a certain profession or activity). This newly established punishment could be imposed on individuals only, but not on legal entities and sole traders. The laws that provide for such punishment are the Forest Act and the Decree for Combating Petty Hooliganism. The content and duration of this punishment are regulated in new art. 16, para. 1 and para 2 of AVPA. According to this legal provision unpaid work is work, performed for the benefit of society without restriction of other rights to punishment. The duration of the penalty may not be less than 40 hours and more than 200 hours per year for not more, than two consecutive years. The procedural rules for imposing this sanction are provided for in art. 47a, art. 58a-58c and art.63a of AVPA. Unpaid work for the benefit of society is imposed only by the court (art.47a of AVPA) and the proceedings before the district court for imposing this punishment are regulated in Art. 58a-58c of AVPA and before the cassation instance in art. 63a of AVPA. While the amendments have not yet entered into force, the following weaknesses and areas of improvement have been preliminary identified in the legal framework:

- If the sanction for the violation includes one or more administrative penalties, the AVPA could provide for clear criteria when the competent authority shall determine the most severe administrative penalty – unpaid work for the benefit of society – and when fine. These criteria shall avoid the sanctioning authority's subjective approach.

- The AVPA could also provide for cases where the enforcement of the penalty unpaid work for the benefit of society should be deferred into two consecutive years, for example when it is longer than a certain duration, when the person works or other similar criteria.
- A prerequisite for the imposition of this type of administrative penalty is that the offence has been repeated or that it is committed systematically. The new provision of § 1 (2) of the Additional Provisions of AVPA states that the repeated violation is committed within one year of the entry into force of an act imposing an administrative penalty for a violation of the same type, unless otherwise provided for in the same act. However, there is not definition of systematic violation in the AVPA. This legislative gap could create difficulties in practice. Such a definition could be:

  > *A systematic violation occurs where three or more administrative violations of the particular law or its implementing acts are committed within one year*

- The proceedings before the district court are intended to be initiated on the initiative of the sanctioning authority. Under Article 58a of the Act, where the administrative offence is punishable by unpaid work for the benefit of society, the official referred to in Article 37 para.1 AVPA shall forward the file to the administrative authority, which shall submit it to the relevant district court for a decision within three days of its receipt. The Act does not provide for the possibility for the sanctioning authority, once it has received the file, to assess its legality in the exercise of its powers under Article 52 para.2 and para. 4 of AVPA. Such a possibility could ensure that the rules of procedure are observed in the pre-judicial stage of the proceedings before assessment by the court.
- The legal framework on evidence before the court also could be improved. The law provides for the possibility of examining witnesses before a court if it considers this to be necessary. But if the court considers the examination of witnesses is not necessary, is it possible to be gathered other sources of evidence, such as written and material evidence and means of evidence and verbal means of evidence obtained by means of explanations of the person against whom the act was drawn up. It is clear that the rules on proof under Article 58b para 6 AVPA are not exhaustive. However, neither Article 58b nor Article 84 AVPA contains a restrictive reference to the Criminal procedural Code or any other procedural regulation to remedy this gap in the law.

More generally, the legislator chose to undertake this reform of the AVPA sanctions system with the introduction of one but the most severe punishment instead of option for a variety of sanctions with different severity. Following the practice of other EU Member States (Box 3.1). The AVPA could provide for other typologies of administrative penalties alternative to the pecuniary sanction in order to ensure that the deterrent goal of the administrative penalty can be realized even if the offenders have no income and the fine cannot be enforced. Indeed, in the vast number of cases the fine remains unpaid, which almost completely eliminates the preventive effect of administrative punishment. In this way the enforcing bodies would have an effective toolkit of alternative sanctions which would enhance its effectiveness and deterrence.

Box 3.1. Typologies of administrative penalties and sanctions in selected EU Member States and EU Law

In some EU Member States, such as Spain, the term administrative sanction (*sanción administrativa*) is used only for punitive sanctions outside criminal law. Next to that, Spanish scholarship distinguishes non-punitive administrative means or acts unfavourable to the citizen (*medidas desfavorables*), which are:

- Restraining measures, such as *multas coercitivas*;
- Measures to restore the infringed legality, such as the withdrawal of a permit;
- Contractual penalties;
- The reimbursement of aids or public grants;
- The cancellation of an administrative concession;
- Surcharges for late payments;
- Administrative fixation of compensation for damage caused by individuals to public property.

In other EU Member States, such as the Netherlands and Germany, similar measures are named administrative sanctions as well. In these systems administrative sanctions are divided between punitive or deterrent administrative sanctions and remedial sanctions. In Austria, Germany, and Spain administrative offenses have a definition exclusively reserved for the transgression an administrative penalty can be imposed for (*Ordnungswidrigkeit, Verwaltungsübertretung* and *infracciones administrativas*).

According to Article 21 of the Code of Administrative Offences of Lithuania, the following penalties may be imposed:

> "1) warning;
>
> *2) a pecuniary sanction;*
>
> *3) items, which was an administrative violation of the instrument or direct object, and income, which were obtained administrative infringement, seizure;*
>
> *4) special rights (the right to drive a vehicle, to fly an aircraft crew member of the aircraft maintenance work of air traffic controller, the right to hunt or to fish, the right to hold the fishing vessel's captain duties, the right to drive inland waterway transport, the right to manage the rolling stock, the right to use or importation of equipment, facilities, radio transmission, radio suppression or radio monitoring devices, the use of electronic communications resources to engage in amateur radio and other radio stations of users activities, the right to hold certain positions seagoing ship rights to design buildings or carry out construction projects expertise) exclusion;*
>
> *5) administrative arrest;*
>
> *6) removal from work (duties).*
>
> *The first part of Article 3-6 points following administrative penalties can only identify laws of the Republic of Lithuania.*
>
> *Lithuanian Republic laws may establish other than those referred to in this article administrative penalties species.*
>
> *The cases provided as an alternative penalty area (city) district court order or other body (official), hearing the cases of administrative violations, the resolution and the offender's consent pecuniary sanction or part thereof may be replaced by no more than 400 hours of free public works, counting one public works free*

> *hour for six euro pecuniary sanction. In this case, the body (official) set a time limit within which the person is required to perform the assigned free public works."*

In the Czech Republic, an administrative punishment under Section 35 of Act No. 250/2016 Coll. can be imposed for an offense and includes:

- Admonition
- pecuniary sanction
- prohibition of activity
- forfeiture of an item or substitute value
- publication of a decision on offense.

In France administrative sanctions can be divided into three categories: moral sanctions, sanctions involving deprivation of rights and pecuniary sanctions.

As regards the "moral sanction", it essentially includes warnings and reprimands. For example, in the fight against doping, the French Anti-Doping Agency may issue a warning to an athlete as a sanction.

With regard to the sanction depriving an athlete of his or her rights, it is mainly the withdrawal of an authorisation or approval that can be imposed on a temporary or permanent basis. It may also consist of a ban on exercising regulated professions and activities.

Finally, as regards financial sanctions, pecuniary sanctions are one of the main administrative sanctions. Several independent administrative authorities have the power to impose pecuniary sanctions. The qualification of "administrative sanction" is generally excluded in the case of police measures, precautionary or preparatory measures and contractual sanctions, since none of them is fundamentally repressive in nature.

From the broader EU perspective, the EU imposes the obligation on Member States to introduce a huge diversity of measures and sanctions of penalties in their legislation. Article 4 and 5 of Regulation 2988/95 offer an illustration of the way EU law makes a distinction between administrative measures, administrative penalties and criminal penalties. Article 4 of this regulation determines which administrative measures may be imposed. This is the withdrawal of the wrongly obtained advantage by the obligation to pay or repay the amounts due or wrongly received, or by the total or partial loss of the security provided in support of the request for a benefit granted or at the time of the receipt of an advance. The fourth paragraph of Article 4 clarifies that these measures are not regarded as penalties. Article 5 of Regulation 2988/95 provides for the administrative penalties that can be imposed. They have to be distinguished from criminal penalties. Article 5, first paragraph, Regulation 2988/95 reads as follows:

> "(1) Intentional irregularities or those caused by negligence may lead to the following administrative penalties:
>
> *(a) payment of an administrative pecuniary sanction;*
>
> *(b) payment of an amount greater than the amounts wrongly received or evaded, plus interest where appropriate ; this additional sum shall be determined in accordance with a percentage to be set in the specific rules, and may not exceed the level strictly necessary to constitute a deterrent;*
>
> *(c) total or partial removal of an advantage granted by Community rules, even if the operator wrongly benefited from only a part of that advantage;*
>
> *(d) exclusion from, or withdrawal of, the advantage for a period subsequent to that of the irregularity;*

> *(e) temporary withdrawal of the approval or recognition necessary for participation in a Community aid scheme;*
>
> *(f) the loss of a security or deposit provided for the purpose of complying with the conditions laid down by rules or the replenishment of the amount of a security wrongly released;*
>
> *(g) other penalties of a purely economic type, equivalent in nature and scope, provided for in the sectoral rules adopted by the Council in the light of the specific requirements of the sectors concerned and in compliance with the implementing powers conferred on the Commission by the Council."*

Finally Austria's Administrative Penalty Act provides the possibility for temporary prison sentence and substitute confinment to prevent people from repeating an administrative offence of similar kind and in case the fine cannot be collected.

> **"Articles 11-12**
>
> *Prison sentence may be imposed only if necessary to prevent culprits from repeating an administrative offence of similar kind.*
>
> *The minimum of prison sentence to be imposed shall be for twelve hours. Prison sentence exceeding a two weeks' term may be imposed only if necessary for particularly aggravating reasons. The maximum prison sentence which may be imposed is for a six weeks' term. In case Article 11 prohibits imposing a prison sentence, the fine imposable for the respective offence in addition to the prison sentence shall be imposed. If no such fine is provided, a fine of up to EUR 2 180 shall be imposed.*
>
> *Article 16*
>
> *Whenever a fine is imposed, also a substitute confinement term shall be determined, in case the fine cannot be collected.*
>
> *The substitute prison sentence must not exceed the maximum possible prison term applicable for the administrative offence and, if prison sentence or anything else is not provided for, it must not exceed two weeks. The maximum admissible substitute prison sentence shall be six weeks. It shall be determined in accordance with the rules applicable for imposing sentences regardless of the provisions of Article 12."*

Source: OECD Research and (European Committee on Crime Problems, 2020[11]).

3.2. Bulgaria could provide for the possibility to impose additional typologies of penalties on sole traders and legal entities, alternatively to or cumulatively with pecuniary sanctions

The liability of legal entities and sole traders for non-fulfilment of an obligation to the state or the municipalities in carrying out their activity leads to a pecuniary sanction, which is the only typology provided for by the legal framework. At the same time, several administrative laws provide for the possibility to impose coercive administrative measures such as the sealing of the commercial site under Art. 124b, para. 1 of the Law on Excise Duties and Tax Warehouses (LEDTW), prohibition for access and removal of the available goods from the site, under Art. 124c, para. 1 of LEDTW, suspension of the validity of the issued license under art. 64, para. 1, item 2 of the Commodity Exchanges and Markets Act. However, there is a clear distinction between coercive administrative measures and administrative penalties, and the former cannot be considered as an alternative to the latter, because they are imposed on different grounds and for different legal purposes. According to Art. 22. AVPA:

> *Applied for prevention and stopping of the administrative violations, as well as for prevention and removal of the harmful consequences from them can be compulsory administrative measures*

Similarly to the natural persons, the absence of alternative options to the pecuniary sanction entails the risk that the imposed pecuniary sanction may not be enforced, for example in a situation where the sole trader and the legal entity do not possess sufficient assets. Therefore, in addition to the penalty payment, Bulgaria could impose other sanctions alternatively or cumulatively with the pecuniary sanction. Considering the practice in other EU countries (Box 3.2), they could be:

- obligation for compensation/compensation for damages
- promulgation of the issued court act
- temporary restriction of the rights of legal entities
- exclusion from tax relief
- suspension or revocation of permits, licenses or concessions related to the violation
- ban on participation in public procurement procedures
- ban on advertising goods and services
- closure of branches, premises and offices of the responsible legal entity.

This would also be in line with the assessment of the OECD Working Group on Bribery in its Phase 4 report, which recommended Bulgaria to amend its legislation to allow for the debarment of legal persons as part of the sanctions against legal persons (OECD, 2021[2])

Box 3.2. Alternative sanctions to legal entities in EU countries

According to an OECD comparative study on responsibility of legal entities for foreign bribery offences, sanctions for legal persons include pecuniary sanctions, confiscation or disgorgement, debarment from public procurement, or other forms of public advantage, and other penalties (e.g. dissolution and publication of sentence). Other examples include the oversight of the legal person's operations and compliance efforts either by the judiciary or by a court-appointed corporate monitor, prohibition on advertising the business (e.g. Poland); and orders for the publication of sentence (e.g. Belgium, Czech Republic, France, Poland and Portugal). Similarly, a Council of Europe study lists the following non-financial penalties in place for legal entities: Exclusion from public subsidies and grants; disqualification from public contracts; annulment of procurement decisions; debarment by development banks; loss of export privileges; ban of activities; supervision; probation and bail; liquidation; public register; publication of judgement. Furthermore, according to both the Second Protocol to the Convention on the Protection of the EU's financial interests and the Framework Decision 2003/568/JHA on combating corruption in the private sector, where an offence covered by such instruments is committed by a head of a legal person, other sanctions may be imposed such as: debarment from public procurement or public aid; temporary or permanent ban on commercial activity; placing under judicial supervision; termination by court order.

As for specific examples in Italy, penalties imposed on the basis of corporate liability under Law 231/2001 include financial penalties, exclusion from public tender processes, confiscation of the proceeds of crime, and publication of the judgment.

In Slovenia provides for a wider range of sanctions than those provided for in the Bulgarian law. For criminal offenses, the following penalties may be imposed on legal persons: (1) a pecuniary sanction; (2) confiscation of property; (3) dissolution of the legal person; (4) prohibition to dispose of the securities held by the legal person.

The pecuniary sanction may vary between EUR 10 000 and EUR 1 000 000. Where the offence has caused damage to foreign property or the legal person has obtained an unlawful property advantage, the upper limit of the pecuniary sanction imposed may be two hundred times the value of the damage or advantage.

Half or more of the property of the legal person or all of its property may be confiscated. Confiscation of property may be imposed for a criminal offence punishable by a penalty of five years' imprisonment or a more severe penalty. In the case of insolvency proceedings as a result of the confiscation of property imposed, creditors may be paid out of the confiscated property.

The dissolution of a legal person may be imposed if the activities of the legal person have been wholly or mainly used to commit criminal offences. In addition to the dissolution of a legal person, the court may order the confiscation of property. Where the penalty of dissolution of a legal person has been imposed, liquidation proceedings are initiated. Creditors may be paid out of the property of a legal person who has been sentenced to dissolution.

Legal persons convicted for certain types of offenses may be subject to an additional penalty prohibiting the disposal of securities held by a legal person and registered in the central register of book-entry securities for a period between one and eight years.

Source: (OECD, 2016[3]); (Council of Europe, 2020[4]); Dimitrova, "Criminal Law Protection of the EU's Financial Interests in Bulgaria".

3.3. Bulgaria could further clarify and differentiate the liability regimes for minor and obviously minor administrative violations based on the degree of social danger of the offence

The institution of minor case of administrative offence is traditional for administrative penalty law. However, until the latest amendments, the AVPA lacked a legal definition of the minor case and the definition of Article 93 para 9 of the Criminal Code was used. The amendment to the AVPA of 22.12.2020 introduced of legal definitions of the 'minor and obviously minor administrative offence':

> *"Minor case" is one, in which the violation, committed by a natural person or non-fulfilment of an obligation by a sole trader or legal entity to the state or municipality, in view of the absence or insignificance of the harmful effects or in view of other mitigating circumstances, constitutes a lower degree of public danger, than ordinary cases of breach or non-performance of an obligation of the kind concerned.*
>
> *A "obviously minor case" of a violation occurs when the act reveals a clearly insignificant degree of public danger.*

The latest amendments to the AVPA, which will enter into force on 23.12.2021, clarify the institute of minor case under article 28 AVPA. A positive change is that the warning can only be written, with a one-year period from the entry into force of the warning. A legislative restriction has also been introduced in Article 29 AVPA, according to which 'The provision of Art. 28 shall not apply to traffic safety violations for all types of transport, committed after use of alcohol, narcotic substances or their analogues'.

Despite these positive developments, the institution of the minor case shall be the subject of future legislative amendments.

A contradiction seems to emerge between the provisions of Article 28 AVPA and Article 39 para. 2 AVPA in so far as it is not clear in which cases the authority may issue a warning and when it can impose a pecuniary sanction of between BGN 10 and BGN 50. Moreover, the confession of the perpetrator, which is traditionally perceived as a mitigating circumstance in the case of Article 39 par.2, aggravates perpetrator's situation. This requires a reconsideration of the provisions of Article 28 of AVPA and Article 39 para 2 of the AVPA which correspond to the concept of a obviously minor case and minor case. It would be appropriate to apply the exemption from administrative responsibility by means of a written warning if the case is obviously minor, as well as to minor cases under Article 39 para of the AVPA and, in other cases, to establish ad hoc offences for minor cases.

These challenges have also been confirmed in the answers to the following question of the OECD questionnaire: "Does the legislation on administrative offences and penalties within your jurisdiction provide for specific provisions for minor or obviously minor cases of administrative offences?" The number of respondents answer this question in the negative, even though they carry out administrative penalty activities on the basis of a number of legal acts. During the interviews conducted, the institution of the minor case referred to in Article 28 AVPA was mentioned as one of the most controversial in the administrative penalty.

One of the few of legislations providing for an ad-hoc offence of minor case of administrative violation is Article 415c of the Labour Code, which establishes administrative responsibility for a minor case, but the penalties provided for are lower than those for offences of the same type, which are not minor. Another such example is set out in Article 126b of Excises and Tax Warehouses Act. But these compositions are exceptions rather than the rule for the differentiation of administrative responsibility. The establishment of ad-hoc offences would be particularly appropriate in regards to violations with high levels of penalties. Since Article 28 AVPA is currently also applicable to such violations, administrative authorities can relieve the offenders from administrative responsibility and to warn the offenders that if they commit another offence, they will be punished. The question therefore arise as to how many and what attenuating circumstances must be present in order for the offender to be exempted from a minimum penalty of BGN 5 000 or BGN 10 000 and whether this is not a prerequisite for the creation of malpractice by the sanctioning authorities and the act issuers. In order this possibility to be overcome, it would be appropriate, in the case of administrative offences which are punishable by penalties with a high minimum threshold, to lay down separate offences for minor cases of administrative offences analogous to Article 415c of the Labour Code, rather than exempting offenders from criminal liability on the basis of Article 28 AVPA. This should be especially the case for infringements characterised by a rich variety of factual indications, since it is precisely when they are implemented that there may be a number of mitigating circumstances which have not been identified as constituent features of the offence. More generally, Bulgaria could establish minor administrative offences in cases of minor case and exempt from administrative liability by means of a written warning only in cases of obviously minor cases. In this way, administrative responsibility will be differentiated according to the degree of social danger of the offences of the same type and the warrant to be provided for as a legal consequence, only for the genuinely lightest cases of violations where the social danger is manifestly negligible.

3.4. Bulgaria could extend the possibility to pay reduced fine to penalties imposed by a judicial decision

Art. 79b of AVPA provides for the possibility to pay a reduced percentage of a fine when the penalty decision is subject to appeal and the infringer refuses to appeal. This article is applicable only where the fine or penalty payment has been imposed by an enforceable decision, which includes two groups of cases: when the penalty is imposed by a penalty order or when the fine is imposed by means of an electronic slip. The slip under art. 39 para 2 and para 2a is not subject to regular judicial review, and if the offender is sanctioned through such article there are no legal grounds for additional 20% discount of the amount of the penalty.

At the same time, the possibility to pay a reduced fine or penalty payment under article 79b should also be possible for persons sanctioned by a judicial decision and not only by penalty order. A fine may be imposed by a judicial decision in two cases: where the proceedings before the court are initiated for a breach that can be sanctioned by a penalty unpaid work for the benefit of the society, in accordance with Articles 58a to 58c of AVPA and culminating in a decision by which the court imposes a fine on the offender; where, in the course of criminal proceedings, the court considers that the act for which the accused person has been held criminally liable is an administrative violation but not a criminal offence and imposes a fine on him, in accordance with Article 301 (4) of the Criminal Procedure Code. In each of these cases, the offender was penalised by a law enforcement act imposing an administrative fine for an administrative offence in an amount individualised by the court. The legal position is therefore identical to that of an offender penalised by a penalty order which has not become final.

Bulgaria could thus allow the infringer penalised by a fine under Article 58b of AVPA or, in accordance with Article 301 (4) of Criminal procedure Code, to also have the possibility to benefit from the privilege of Article 79b of the AVPA and, within the time limit for appeal against the court's decision, be able to pay the fine in a reduced amount.

3.5. Bulgaria could improve the uniformity of administrative penalties in special laws and consider reforming the system of sanctions

The principle of proportionality between the administrative violation and the administrative penalty is a fundamental principle in the administrative penalty law. This principle is guaranteed both in the construction of the *corpus delicti* of administrative violations and in the enforcement of the legal framework.

When the administrative penalty does not take into account the gravity of the offence, even strict adherence to the legal framework by the enforcing authorities does not guarantee that the penalty will be proportionate to the offence, which in its turn may lead to disproportionate sanctions.

Weaknesses in the legal framework related to the differentiation of administrative penalties fall into several different categories that are addressed in the following sections. Based on the domestic and comparative analysis, these difficulties could be overcome in two alternative ways: one option is modifying the special laws being affected by inappropriate levels of sanctions such as the ones pointed out in each section. Alternatively, perhaps in the longer term, Bulgaria could consider reforming the system of sanctions, setting a limited number of sanction ranges and then having each old and special law deciding the applicable ranges depending on the choice of the legislator. Box 3.3 provides an example of the latter model adopted by the Netherlands as well as of a reform that simplified the level of sanction in special laws of the Czech Republic.

Box 3.3. Unity and harmonisation of legislation concerning administrative penalties in the Netherlands, Czech Republic and Germany

Many countries struggle with the development of administrative offenses in special laws and the position of the general laws. The development of the Social Welfare State and European Law are seen as some of the causes of the expansion of administrative offenses in special laws. This causes some kind of a centrifugal force creating many deviations from the general code or general laws. This force can be counterbalanced with an effective policy of legislative quality, consisting of elements such as directives and guidance, models etc.

In the Netherlands a system of 6 categories to determine the maximum pecuniary sanction in criminal law was introduced. These categories were introduced in article 23 of the Dutch Criminal Code, which reads as follows:

"**Article 23 Dutch Criminal Code**

3. The maximum pecuniary sanction that can be imposed for an offense shall be equal to the amount of the category determined for that offense.

4. There are six categories:

- the first category, EUR 435
- the second category, EUR 4 350
- the third category, EUR 8 700
- the fourth category, EUR 21 750
- the fifth category, EUR 87 000
- the sixth category, EUR 870 000.

5. For a violation or a crime for which no pecuniary sanction has been imposed, a pecuniary sanction may be imposed up to a maximum of the amount of the first or third category respectively.

6. For a violation or a crime for which a pecuniary sanction has been imposed, but for which no pecuniary sanction category has been determined, a pecuniary sanction may be imposed up to a maximum of the amount of the first or third category, respectively, if this amount is higher than the amount of the pecuniary sanction imposed for the offense in question.

7. If a legal person is convicted, if the pecuniary sanction category determined for the offense does not permit appropriate punishment, a pecuniary sanction may be imposed up to a maximum of the amount of the next higher category. If a pecuniary sanction of the sixth category can be imposed for the act and that pecuniary sanction category does not permit appropriate punishment, a pecuniary sanction can be imposed up to a maximum of 10% of the annual turnover of the legal person in the financial year prior to the judgment or punishment order.

8. The preceding paragraph applies mutatis mutandis to a conviction of a company without legal personality, partnership, shipping company or special purpose capital.

9. The amounts referred to in the fourth paragraph are adjusted every two years, with effect from 1 January of a year, by order in council to the development of the consumer price index since the previous adjustment of these amounts. In this adjustment, the monetary amount of the first category is rounded down to a multiple of EUR 5 and, on the basis of the monetary amount of this first category and while maintaining the mutual relationship between the amounts of the pecuniary sanction categories, the amounts of the second to and determined by the sixth pecuniary sanction category."

The 1983 legislation not only introduced this general provision, it also altered almost all special laws in order to bring them in line with the new provisions in the general code. Despite this effort to bring all special laws in line with the new general provision, this general provision still has two safety net provisions in paragraph 5 and of article 23 DCC.

The general regulation of administrative pecuniary sanctions was part of the legislative project to build the General Administrative Law Act (Algemene wet bestuursrecht). This was done in building blocks called tranches. Every building block was based upon an analysis of the general administrative issue involved and the different provisions on that issue in special laws. The choices of the legislator were proposed in the supplement of GALA in the building block, and a separate bill provided for all alterations (hundreds of them) necessary to bring special legislation in line with the general provisions on the same legal issue.

Following this legislative strategy the general provisions on administrative pecuniary sanctions were added to GALA and more than 120 acts providing for the power to impose an administrative pecuniary sanctions were altered.

Despite proposals to add such a provision, the legislator did not provide for a system to determine the maximum administrative pecuniary sanction in a way similar to article 23 DCC. This meant the centrifugal forces got claws on the determination of maximum pecuniary sanctions in special acts, resulting in pecuniary sanctions that got higher and higher. By now the special legislator has to fix the maxima of administrative pecuniary sanctions according to the categories of article 23 DCC. This obligation is provided for in the directives of the Prime Minister mentioned above. This directive reads as follows:

"**Directive 5.43**

1. When determining a maximum administrative pecuniary sanction, reference is made to one of the pecuniary sanction categories in the Criminal Code, unless it is necessary to link up with deviating amounts in an existing system.

2. The following model is used for the determination in which a maximum administrative pecuniary sanction is set:

The administrative pecuniary sanction to be imposed on the basis of [article ... / the articles ...] shall not exceed the amount determined for the [...] category, referred to in [article 23, fourth paragraph, of the Code. of Criminal Law.

3. If, due to the deterrent effect or major financial interests, it is necessary to be able to impose a very high administrative pecuniary sanction on companies that is in line with the highest pecuniary sanction category in the Criminal Code or that, if that is more, is related to the turnover of the company concerned, the following model is used:

The administrative pecuniary sanction to be imposed on the basis of [article ... / the articles ...] shall not exceed the amount determined for the sixth category, referred to in [article 23, fourth paragraph, of the Criminal Code] or if this is more, no more than 10% of the turnover of the company or, if the violation was committed by an association of undertakings, of the combined turnover of the companies that are part of the association, in the financial year preceding the decision in which the administrative pecuniary sanction is imposed."

Explanation

First paragraph. In administrative law, the maximum amount of administrative pecuniary sanctions is set at an amount that is comparable to one of the pecuniary sanction categories of Article 23, fourth paragraph, of the Criminal Code (Article 27, fourth paragraph, of the Criminal Code BES). Due to the dynamic reference, the amounts are regularly indexed.

Third paragraph. In a number of legislative complexes, the maximum amount is not fixed, but is related to the turnover (see, for example, Article 57 of the Competition Act, Article 85 of the Healthcare Market Regulation Act and Article 1:82 of the Financial Supervision Act). Such an open maximum pecuniary sanction is acceptable, provided that good arguments can be given for this, such as the different sizes of companies."

The Act on Working Hours provides an example among many:

"Article 10:7 Act on Working Hours

1. The administrative pecuniary sanction that can be imposed for a violation does not exceed the amount of the fifth category, referred to in Article 23, fourth paragraph, of the Criminal Code.

2 Without prejudice to the first paragraph, the official designated on the basis of Article 10:5, first or second paragraph, increases the administrative pecuniary sanction to be imposed by 100% of the pecuniary sanction, determined on the basis of the sixth paragraph, if within a period of five years prior on the day of discovery of the violation an earlier violation, consisting of non-compliance with the same

legal obligation or prohibition or non-compliance with similar obligations and prohibitions to be designated by or pursuant to order in council, has been established and the administrative pecuniary sanction for the previous violation has become irrevocable."

In the Czech Republic, one of the reasons to re-codify the misdemeanours and other administrative offenses in the Czech Republic in 2017 was the proliferation of administrative offenses in special laws. The Act 251/2016 on Certain Misdemeanours regulates several specific misdemeanours, and Act 183/2017 modified the approximately 250 special laws in order to eliminate provisions contrary to the new regulations. One of the results was that many administrative offenses in special laws were converted into misdemeanours according to the general act 250/2016. The end result was simplification of the system.

Similarly, in German criminal law, the Act to introduce the new Criminal Code (Einführungsgesetz zum Strafgesetzbuch (EGStGB)) of 2 March 1974 changed special legislation to bring that legislation in conformity with the change of the criminal code from a system of three types of crimes (*Übertretungen*, *Verbrechen* and *Vergehen*) into a system of two, with the lightest category of criminal acts being transferred to that system of administrative penalties, and taken out of criminal law. This legislative choice was designed by a change of the Criminal Code (the general act) and an act changing special legislation in order to bring that special legislation in conformity with the general act.

Source: OECD Research.

3.5.1. Special laws could reduce the use of fixed penalties, which do not allow proportionality and the differentiation of the punishment

In some areas of legal regulation, such as transport safety, and in particular for speeding offences, fixed penalties do not lead to the imposition of inappropriate penalties. These violations consist of speeding and the pecuniary sanction increases directly in proportion to the increase in speeding. In other words, the *corpus delicti* of the violation is not characterised by a variety of objective and subjective elements and a number of non-constituent, mitigating and aggravating circumstances that reduce or diminish social danger of the violation cannot be exhibited. However, fixed penalties should be used in a limited way. Such penalties are appropriate only where the infringement is not characterised by a variety of factual indicia relevant to its social danger and where the essential element of the violation that increases or decreases the social danger of violation may be graded or lead to a graduation of the flat-rate penalty (which is the increase in the speed, the penalties for this type of infringement being increased in proportion to the increase in speed).

In other laws, where the social danger of the offence varies and can be shown to be lower or higher, a fixed penalty is a legal impediment to the differentiation and individualisation of the penalty. Thus, the violations with different levels of social danger are punishable by the same penalty. For example, Article 67 para 2 of the Renewable Energy Act provides that: 'A distributor who markets liquid fuels of petroleum origin in breach of Article 47 (2) or (3) shall be liable to a pecuniary sanction of BGN 50 000 or a financial penalty of BGN 100 000. The penalty provision shall refer to the rules of conduct in Article 47 (2) and (3) which have been infringed, but each of these infringements has its own social danger. The fixed penalty of BGN 50 000 for natural persons and 100 000 for legal entities does not allow the quantity of liquid fuels offered to be taken into account, nor the period during which these fuels are marketed, facts and circumstances relevant to the social danger degree of the violation. Penalties are also fixed in the Road Transport Act, although often the same provision contains multiple violation, whose degree of social danger may vary. In those legal acts, it is not appropriate to lay down fixed penalties, but relevantly defined sanctions.

The fixed amount of the penalty is not appropriate in the case of the so-called general provisions laying down penalties. For example, Article 185 of the Road Traffic Act establishes that a pecuniary sanction of BGN 20 shall be imposed for any violation of this Act and of the legal instruments issued on the basis of this Act, for which no other penalty is provided for.

Furthermore, the fixed amount of the penalty is not an appropriate option in cases where evaluation features are included in the legal composition of the violation. For example, Article 177 par.4 of the Road Traffic Act provides:

> *(4) (New - SG 2/18, in force from 20.05.2018) Whoever manages a road vehicle with unsecured cargo in violation of the requirements of the ordinance under Art. 127, Para. 4, shall be pecuniary sanctioned:*
>
> *1. BGN 500 - in case of established minor deficiencies in securing the cargo;*
>
> *2. BGN 1 000 - in case of established major deficiencies in securing the cargo;*
>
> *3. BGN 1 500 - in case of established dangerous deficiencies in securing the cargo.*

The features of 'minor, major and dangerous deficiencies' are open to interpretation and may be different in nature and type, which would increase or reduce social danger of the concrete violation. It is therefore appropriate, in this and other similar situations, the penalty to be determined relatively.

Apart from that, the fixed amount of the pecuniary sanction or proprietary sanction, in particular where it is high, renders that penalty impossible in practice. In the example given, if a legal entity does not own property and money, such penalties cannot be enforced. This problem has also been identified in other legislative acts, for example, for an infringement under Article 182 of the Tourism Act, the penalty is fixed without taking into account the possibility that the violation actually committed may present a lower or higher degree of danger to society.

Last but not least, the fixed amount of the sanction creates difficulties in a possible appeal of the penal order before the court, which can be appealed solely on the basis of the manifest injustice of the penalty, without calling into question the fact of the offence committed and the personality of the offender.

The problem of fixed sanctions is also related to the more general problem of the penalty system, which includes too few penalties, as well as to the mandatory prohibition of replacing one penalty with another penalty in Article 27 par.4 AVPA (except in the cases referred to in Article 15 par.2 of the Act — where the penalty provided for is a pecuniary sanction and the offender is a minor).

3.5.2. Special laws could reduce the wide range between the minimum and maximum penalty for a particular type of violation and the regulation of multiple administrative violations in a single legal provision with the same sanction, without taking into account the degree of social danger of the violations

The analysis of the legislation and the replies received in the course of the survey show a link between these two weaknesses in the legal framework. Very often, the establishment of multiple administrative offences in a single provision is accompanied by a wide range of penalties. These weaknesses will therefore be addressed jointly.

The special minimum and the special maximum of the sanction shall be the legal assessment of the lowest and highest possible degree of social danger of violation of the same type. Therefore, if the sanction is too wide, this would make it more difficult for the penalty to be properly differentiated based on proportionality and risk and would create the conditions for misapplication of the law.

A clear example of this weakness in the legal framework is Article 273. par. 1 item 9 of Act on the Operation of the Collective Investment Schemes and of other Undertakings for Collective Investment: 'Whoever commits or allows the committing of the offense of: 9. (new - SG 76/16, in force from 30.09.2016, previous item 8, amend. and suppl. - SG 102/19) Art. 4, Para. 5 and 6, Art. 6, para. 4 and 5, Art. 7, para. 2 and 3, Art. 9, para. 1 and 2, Art. 10, para. 5, Art. 10a, Art. 17, para. 2, Art. 18, para. 1, Art. 37, Para. 8, Art. 48, para. 3 and 4, Art. 52, Art. 57, para. 1, 5 -10, Art. 58, para. 2, Art. 59, art. 61, para. 1 and 2, Art. 62, 63, art. 65, para. 1-3, Art. 78, para. 4 and 5, Art. 79, Art. 81, para. 2, Art. 91, Para. 1 and 3, Art. 93, para. 1, 2, 4 and 5, Art. 94, para. 1 and 2, Art. 98, para. 2, Art. 194, Para. 4, Art. 197, Para. 11, Art. 216, Para. 5, shall be punished with a pecuniary sanction from BGN 1 000 to 5 000 000;

Another example is Article 210a of the Consumer Protection Act, which has established that for violations of Art. 68c, Art. 68d, para 1 and 2, Art. 68g, items 1 – 11, 13, 15, 18 – 23 and Art. 68k, items 3 – 6 to the guilty person a pecuniary sanction in amount from BGN 500 to BGN 15 000 shall be imposed, and the sole traders and legal entities – a proprietary sanction in the amount from BGN 1 000 to BGN 30 000.

It is clear that the minimum limit of the penalty is thirty times lower than its maximum. At the same time, Article 210a of the of the Consumer Protection Act refers to a number of rules laid down in Articles 68c, 68d, 68 g and Article 68k of the Act. The referral technique aims at legislative savings and is applied in strict compliance with the Act on Normative Acts rules. However, where that legislative technique creates grounds for infringement of the principle of proportionality and the individualisation of the punishment, priority should be given to the question of the principle that the seriousness of the offence committed must correspond to the severity of the administrative penalty imposed. More than thirty individual violations referred to in Articles 68c, 68d, 68 g (11) to (1), 13, 15, 18, -23 and Article 68k (3) to (6) of the Act, but for each of these many violations with varying degrees of social danger, the sanctioning authority may impose a pecuniary sanction of BGN 500 to BGN 15 000.

Art. 221, par. 1, item 2 of Public Offering of Securities Act provides that whoever commits or admits commitment of violation of: Art. 77b, para. 5, Art. 77e, para. 7, Art. 89i, para. 2, 3 and 4, Art. 89k, para. 3, Art. 89m, Art. 89c, para. 1 and 2, Art. 89t, para. 1 and 2, Art. 100a, para. 2 and 3, Art. 100b, para. 3, 5, 7 and 8, Art. 100f, Art. 100g, para. 4, Art. 100i, Art. 100k, para. 3, Art. 100p, para. 2 and 3, 100t, 100u, Art. 100x, al. 3 and 5, Art. 100y, para. 1, 2, 3, 5, 6 and 7, Art. 100z, para. 2 and 3, Art. 110, para. 6, para. 7, sentence two and para. 9, Art. 110c, para. 1 - 3, Art. 110d, Art. 111, para. 6, sentences one and two, Art. 112b, para. 12, Art. 115, para. 1, 2, 4 - 8, 10 and 12, Art. 115a, Art. 115b, Art. 115c, para. 4 and 5, Art. 116d, para. 3, 5 and 7, Art. 116, para. 3, 5 - 7, Art. 116a, para. 2 - 7 and Art. 116a1, Art. 116c, para. 1 - 7, Art. 117, Art. 118, para. 3, sentence two, Art. 120a, para. 1 - 3, Art. 122, para. 3, Art. 131a, Art. 151, para. 3 - 6, Art. 151a, para. 4, Art. 154, para. 1 and 3, Art. 155, para. 5, Art. 157, Art. 157a, para. 7, shall be punished with a pecuniary sanction in the amount of BGN 1 000 to 2 000.

These examples show that this weakness of the legal framework is not an exception, but is found in a number of administrative laws. It would be appropriate to differentiate liability by creating separate sets of offences and providing for penalties with a narrower range. Apart from this, when it comes to sanctioning offences of the same type, it is appropriate to create, instead of such extensive sanctions, a system of heavier and lighter offences of the same type, thus differentiating penalties.

Another major weakness of the special legislation is that for multiple violations, only natural persons are subject to liability. In a number of situations, the nature of the offence does not make it possible to do so in the form of a failure to fulfil an obligation towards the state or municipalities. For example, the infringement under Article 80 par.5 of the Bulgarian Identity Documents Act, as well as many other violations by definition, can only be committed by a natural person.

However, in a number of situations, failure to comply with an administrative obligation can be both an administrative offence and a failure to fulfil an obligation towards the State and municipalities. In such cases, there is no reasonable justification for making only natural persons subject to administrative responsibility. In these situations, it is appropriate to extend the category of persons subject to administrative responsibility in the same or separate provision, using legal techniques: "a pecuniary sanction or proprietary sanction shall be imposed on ..."

3.5.3. Special laws could reduce the excessively narrow range between the special minimum and the special maximum of the administrative penalties

The too narrow range between the special minimum and the special maximum of the sanction manifests itself as a weakness of the legal framework in cases of reference to a number of rules of law, where possible violations are of varying degrees of public danger. For the sake of legislative economy, some violations are listed too broadly and the limits of sanctions are too narrow, which does not allow enforcement authorities to determine the penalty correctly. It is very often the case that the sanction provision refers to a whole legal act or to a number of legal acts.

For example, in art. 147, para 1 from Civil Aviation Act it is established that: *"Unless duly provided otherwise, for any other violation of this Act, or of the Rules and Regulations for the implementation thereof, the culpable persons shall be penalised by a pecuniary sanction in the amount from BGN 100 to BGN 500."* Regardless of the subsidiary nature of the provision, which applies if no other penalty is provided for the violation, the question remains whether the public danger of the violations provided by the law and regulations is properly assessed and whether by imposing a pecuniary sanction of BGN 100 to 500, the principle of proportionality will be observed.

The narrow range between the special minimum and the special maximum of the sanction is not appropriate in the following situations:

- In the case of blankets and referrals of administrative offences — using the legislative technique of referring to a number of rules in the same or other legal acts, possible infringements are of varying degrees of social danger. It is a common hypothesis that the penalty rule refers to all or many pieces of legislation. This leads to difficulties in the individualisation of the penalty, as violations present varying degrees of social danger.
- In cases where, for reasons of legislative economy, the *corpus delicti* of violation are described too generally and the limits of sanctions are too narrow, which does not allow sanctioning authorities to determine correctly the penalty.

Therefore, sanctions with a narrow range between the minimum and the maximum can only be used as an alternative to fixed sanctions, or for violations that do not have a variety of features.

3.5.4. Special laws could reduce the provision of penalties without a special minimum, as well as of penalties with a very low special minimum

A number of laws do not establish a special minimum sanction. In these cases, the question arises as to the minimum amount of administrative penalty that the enforcement authority may impose. Indeed, a similar approach is observed when outlining the sanctioning part of the criminal law provisions of the Special Part of the Criminal Code, which contains the components of crimes and the penalties provided for them. However, the General Part of the Penal Code regulates the minimum and maximum amounts of each of the types of penalties that are subject to quantitative measurement, which is why, whenever the Special Part of the Criminal Code does not provide for a special minimum, it is the minimum in the General part which applies.

The AVPA lays down a minimum and maximum penalty only with regard to the penalties of deprivation of the right to exercise a particular profession or activity and the penalty provided for by the latest amendments to the AVPA — unpaid work for the benefit of society. However, the AVPA lacks a minimum amount of the most frequently imposed penalty, that is, the administrative pecuniary sanction, as regulated in the Penal Code. This further hampers law enforcement officers in individualising the amount of the type of administrative penalties. This problem is particularly serious where the penalty lacks a special minimum and the special maximum is high, for example for the violations under Article 49 par.1 of Foreigners in the Republic of Bulgaria Act.

> *With a pecuniary sanction up to BGN 3 000 shall be punished a foreigner who: 1. (amend. - SG 97/16) uses invalid passport or another document for travelling substituting it;*
>
> *2. (suppl., SG 42/01; amend. – SG 82/06; suppl. - SG 36/09) loses, damages or demolishes Bulgarian identity document, residence permit or documents issued by the services for border passport-visa control; 3. as captain or member of the crew of a sailing vessel does not observe the established border and passport regime of ports and port towns; 4. (amend. – SG 29/07) does not implement his obligations of art. 17, para. 2 and of art. 30; 5. (amend. – SG 82/09) gives or accepts as pawn or concedes a personal document.*

There are several possible solutions to this problem:

- Establishing a minimum amount of the pecuniary sanction and proprietary sanction in the AVPA;
- Legislative change in the sanctions of special laws, which do not contain minimum amounts of the pecuniary sanction and proprietary sanction.

The first approach could be extremely useful in subsequent codification, but it should only be used when the maximum level of the penalty is not too high. Hypothetically, if a penalty of up to BGN 5 000 is imposed for an offence and there is no special minimum, it is extremely inappropriate to apply a possible special minimum of BGN 100. At the same time, it is perfectly reasonable to apply a possible special minimum of BGN 100 in the AVPA for penalties with a special maximum of BGN 500, which do not contain a special minimum.

The second approach is more difficult to implement in practice because it requires a series of legislative changes to specific legislation involving more than 300 laws and multiple secondary legislation containing administrative penalty provisions. However, its use will make it possible, when differentiating penalties, to take into account the typical degree of social danger of violation of the type concerned and, not least, to rank the special minimum and maximum penalties according to the penalties for other violation of the same legal act.

3.6. The legal framework could provide more objective elements to distinguish between similar criminal and administrative offences

The distinction and differences between crimes and administrative offences is a debated issues in Bulgaria and at the international level. In particular, the problem of "competition" between the *corpus delicti* of administrative offences and *corpus delicti* of the crime arises when they affect the same object, i.e. harm the same type of public relations. That problem arises as regards the legal qualification of the act by the administrative authorities and courts, not in all cases, but only where the characteristic of the legal *corpus delicti* which distinguishes the crime from the offence is assessable. For example, Article 234 (1) of the Penal Code establishes that the distribution or keeping of excise goods without a tax stamp in non-minor cases is a criminal offence and, in other cases, an infringement under Article 123 par. 1 Excises and Tax Warehouses Act. The criterion of 'non-minor case' is the only difference between the criminal offence referred to in Article 234 (1) of the Penal Code and the infringement under Article 123 par. 1 Excises and Tax Warehouses Act. This creates difficulties in practice and causes for a different interpretation of the term 'non-minor case'. Thus, in practice, a criminal authority may qualify the act as a criminal offence and another enforcement authority may qualify that act as an administrative offence.

Similarly, the question arises as to the legal qualification of the hooliganism, which can be qualified as 'petty hooliganism' within the meaning of the Decree on combating petty hooliganism or as a criminal offence under Article 325 of the Criminal Code.

Another example of competition between administrative and criminal liability is the offence under Article 53 par.1 of the Roads Act and the offence referred to in Article 216 par.1 of the Criminal Code, which establishes criminal liability for the destruction or damage of foreign property. In that merger, the criterion for differentiation is a legal criterion 'if the act does not constitute a criminal offence', but there is no constituent element to determine whether the act is an administrative offence or a criminal offence. Similarly, Article 290 (1) (6) of the ZPFI provides for a pecuniary sanction for the person who presents false information or documents if the act does not constitute a document offence. The competition between administrative and criminal liability can be seen in customs smuggling, the Excise Duties and Tax Warehouses Act, the Civil Aviation Act (Article 143 (1) (4) of the ZGV), etc.

In such cases, it is appropriate to establish an objective indication in both special administrative legislation and the Criminal Code of the constituent elements of the offence, serving as a clear criterion for distinguishing between a criminal offence and an administrative offence of the same type. Such an indication may be the value of the object or damage caused by the interception or a special means of committing the act, or conditions of time, place and environment, thus establishing a clearer boundary between criminal offences and administrative offences and overcoming a number of difficulties in the legal qualification of the acts.

3.7. Bulgaria could introduce provisions in special laws to establish penalties for violations, in respect of which no separate sanction is provided for

Administrative violations and penalties have been identified in hundreds of laws and regulations. This creates the risk that some violations of administrative rules will not result in a sanction. For these cases the AVPA establishes the provisions of art. 31 and Art. 32, which are applicable to violations of the bylaws, as well as for non-compliance with orders and other acts of authority of the administrative bodies. This approach deserves support, as it ensures the realisation of liability for infringements for which no sanctions have been imposed. The only problem is the differentiation of responsibility, as in art. 31 of the AVPA which establishes a sanction from BGN 2to BGN 50, with an extremely low special minimum.

Firstly, Bulgaria could raise the amount of sanctions in Articles 31 and 32 order to ensure their meaningfulness and deterrent effect (Box 3.4).

Box 3.4. Proposal for updated ranges of sanctions for breaches without specific penalties

"Art. 31. (Amend., SG 59/92; SG 102/95; SG 11/98) Who does not fulfil or violates a lawful order or ordinance of a body of the authority, including in connection with the economic measures of the state shall be fined by BNG 50 to BNG 200.

Art. 32.

(1) (Amend., SG 59/92; SG 102/95; SG 11/98; SG 25/02) Who does not fulfil or violates an order, a decree or another act issued or adopted by the Council of Ministers, unless the act represents a crime, or other administrative violation shall be fined by BGN 100 to BNG 2 000.

(2) (New, SG 24/87; Amend., SG 59/92; SG 102/95; SG 11/98; Suppl., SG 114/99, in force from January 31 2000; Amend., SG 25/02; Amend., SG 61/02) Who does not fulfil or violates an act according to para 1, related to the accountancy, taxation, customs, foreign currency or ecological legislation, unless the act represents a crime or other administrative violation shall be fined by BGN 400 to BNG 3 000.

(3) (New, SG 67/99; in force from August 27, 1999) If a civil servant, in carrying out the public employment does not fulfil or violates obligations ensuing from the acts under para 1 and 2 shall be fined by BNG 100 to BNG 300."

Source: OECD proposal.

Secondly, Bulgaria could also introduce provisions analogous to those of art. 31 and art. 32 of the AVPA in the special legislation to establish sanctions for violations, in respect of which no separate sanction is provided for. This is because the degree of social danger of specific types of violation may vary and ranges established by Articles 31 and 32 may not be adequate and proportionate to the breach.

For example, the Road Transport Act states in Article 105 par.1 that

> *Infringements of this Act and of secondary legislation issued on the basis thereof, with the exception of the requirements for the transport of dangerous goods for which no other penalty is imposed, shall be punishable by a pecuniary sanction or a pecuniary sanction of BGN 200.*

Paragraphs 2 and 3 also contain general provisions:

> *(2) Infringements of the requirements for the transport of dangerous goods for which no other penalty is imposed shall be punishable by a pecuniary sanction of BGN 500.*
>
> *(3) A driver who, upon inspection by the supervisory authorities, fails to submit a document required by this Act or a regulatory act issued on the basis of this Act, unless otherwise provided, shall be liable to a pecuniary sanction of BGN 50.*

The only disadvantage of those rules is that the penalties are fixed and the respective violations committed may vary in the degree of social danger. Therefore, the general provisions of the laws which lay down sanctions for violations for which no other penalty is provided should be defined in relation to the minimum and maximum sanction provided for by each special law. The minima of these penalties may be adjusted to the minimum level of the penalty laid down in the relevant law and the maximum amounts around the average for infringements of the law.

3.8. Special laws could contain provisions for sanctioning administrative violations committed repeatedly and systematically

With the latest amendments to the AVPA in Article 13 par. 2 of AVPA it is provided that an administrative offence, repeated or systematic, may be punished for via unpaid work for the benefit of the public, imposed independently or at the same time as another penalty referred to in paragraph 1. In Para. 1 (1) item 6 and para 6 of the Additional Provisions of the AVPA definitions of the same type of offence and repeated offence are introduced.

Although these legislative changes strengthen the legal framework, they do not overcome the different approaches of administrative laws with regard to repeated and systematic infringements. These gaps in the law give rise to situations in which, even though the offence is repeated or systematically committed, it is not punished more seriously, because there is no relevant legal provision providing for repeated or systematic offence. The analysis of the specific legislation also shows inconsistencies in the differentiation of sanctions. In some laws, the repeated violation is punishable by a double pecuniary sanction. For example, Article 183 par. 1 of the Tourism Act provides that:

> *Tour-operator or travel agent, who carries out tourist activity in a premise, which fails to meet the requirements or the Ordinance under Art. 64 shall be imposed by a pecuniary sanction in the amount of BGN 100 to 500. According to par.2 'For a repeated breach, the pecuniary sanction shall be in the amount of BGN 200 to 1000.*

Another example is Article 178a par. 4 and 5 of the Road Traffic Act. According to para. 4:

> *A pecuniary sanction amounting to BGN 1000 shall be imposed to a person granted permission under Art. 148, Para 2, which: 1. fails to file a notification or a document certifying the performance of periodical checks with the competent authorities; 2. as a result of the inappropriate storage of documents certifying the performance of periodical checks for technical fitness of road vehicles has allowed their loss, theft or damage.*

According to para. 5

> *In cases of repeated offence under Para 4 the pecuniary sanction shall amount to BGN 2 000.*

Another example are the punishments under Article 143 para 1 of the Civil Aviation Act — for a first violation the sanction is of BGN 3 000 to BGN 10 000, and for a repeated violation under art. 146, the sanction is of BGN 4 000 to BGN 13 000. According to article 224 par.1 of the Wine and Spirit Drinks Act: "When the violations referred to in Articles 201 to 223 are repeated, the amount of the pecuniary sanctions or financial penalties shall be doubled."

However, in a number of cases, the penalty for the repeated offence is three to four times more severe. For example, Article 178 g para 1 of the Road Traffic Act provides for:

> *Punishable by deprivation of the right to drive a motor vehicle for a period of 3 months and a pecuniary sanction of 1 000 BGN shall be any driver who drives in emergency stopping lane of a motorway without the exceptions under Art. 58, Item 3 or in the opposite traffic lane on a motorway and express road.' According to par. 2 'For a repeated offense under par. 1, the punishment shall be deprivation of the right to drive a motor vehicle for a period of 6 months and a pecuniary sanction of BGN 4 000.'*

Other examples may be given in this respect. For violations under Article 53 par.1 of the Roads Act, the penalty shall be BGN 1 000 to BGN 5 000 but for repeated violation - from BGN 2 000 to BGN 7 000. In accordance with Article 54 par. 2 of the Roads Act, where the offence is committed by legal entity and sole trader, the penalty shall be between BGN 4 000 and BGN 12 000. The analysis of the legislation shows that, in some cases, the penalty for repeated violations is even lower than the penalty for the first infringement of the same type. For example, for violations under Article 178 par.1, items 1 to 11 of the Road Traffic Act, the penalty for the first violation is BGN 2 000 to BGN 7 000, and Article 178 para 2 provides that when the offence referred to in paragraph 1 item 6 and item 10 is repeated, the penalty shall be a pecuniary sanction of BGN 1 000 to BGN 5 000 and a withdrawal of the permit. A possible reason for this is the different time period in which the two provisions, including sanctions for them, have been amended, but this and other similar examples point to the need for a uniform approach to repeated and systematic infringements, which are systematically regulated in the AVPA, along with the penalty rules. This approach would be particularly appropriate for future codification of legislation.

Another possible solution is that each special law may lay down its own provisions for repeated offences, the penalty being twice or doubled length, but not more that the AVPA provided for, and for violations of systematic commission the penalty should be three times, or three times longer, but not more than the maximum penalty provided for in the AVPA.

In considering these two options, Bulgaria could also take into account the experience of other EU countries which have specific provisions on recurrent and systemic violations (Box 3.5).

Box 3.5. Recurrent and systemic violations in Austria, Germany, the Netherlands and Spain

Provisions on concurrence and cumulating of penalties are important elements of the principle of proportionality regarding the severity of penalties and punishments. The amount of the administrative pecuniary sanction needs to be in conformity with that proportionality requirement.

The legal systems of administrative penalties in Austria (§ 22 VwSG), Germany (§ 19- § 21 OWiG), the Netherlands, Spain (31 LRJSP), have provisions on concurrence and cumulating of administrative penalties. The legislation in Austria and Germany has provisions dealing with transgressions that fall within legal provisions of both criminal offenses and administrative offenses. These provisions read as follows:

"§ 22 Verwaltungsstrafgesetz (Austria)

(1) Unless the administrative regulations stipulate otherwise, an act is only punishable as an administrative offense if it does not constitute a criminal offense falling within the jurisdiction of the courts.

(2) If someone has committed several administrative offenses through several independent acts or if an act falls under several non-mutually exclusive threats of punishment, the penalties are to be imposed side by side. The same applies if administrative offenses coincide with other criminal acts to be punished by an administrative authority."

"§ 19 Ordnungswidrigkeitengesetz (Germany)

(1) If the same act violates several laws according to which it can be punished as an administrative offense, or such a law several times, only a single pecuniary sanction is imposed.

(2) If several laws are violated, the pecuniary sanction is determined according to the law that threatens the highest pecuniary sanction. The side effects threatened in the other law can be recognised."

"§ 20 Ordnungswidrigkeitengesetz (Germany)

If more than one pecuniary sanction is imposed, each pecuniary sanction shall be assessed separately."

"§ 21 Ordnungswidrigkeitengesetz (Germany)

(1) If an act is both a criminal offense and an administrative offense, only the criminal law is applied. The side effects threatened in the other law can be recognised.

(2) In the case of paragraph 1, however, the act can be punished as an administrative offense if a penalty is not imposed."

"Article 31 LRJSP Concurrence of sanctions (Spain)

1. Acts that have been criminally or administratively punishable may not be punished, in cases where the identity of the subject, fact and foundation is appreciated.

2. When an organ of the European Union has imposed a sanction for the same facts, and provided that the identity of the subject and foundation does not concur, the competent organ to resolve it must take it into account for the purpose of graduating which, in its case, must impose, being able to reduce it, without prejudice to declaring the commission of the infraction."

On the other hand, repeating a similar offense, recidivism, is considered a more serious variety of committing the latter offense. Without legal provision this could lead to a higher penalty within the general maximum of the penalty which is provided for in legislation.

According to the Spanish regulation of administrative penalties in Ley 40/2015 the continuity or persistence in the offending conduct as well as recidivism are elements of the principle of proportionality applicable to the administrative penalty. This principle is codified in article 29 LRJSP which reads as follows:

1. "Administrative sanctions, whether or not of a pecuniary nature, may in no case imply, directly or indirectly, deprivation of liberty.
2. The establishment of pecuniary sanctions must provide that the commission of the typified offenses is not more beneficial for the offender than compliance with the infringed rules.
3. In the normative determination of the sanctioning regime, as well as in the imposition of sanctions by the Public Administrations, the due suitability and necessity of the sanction to be imposed and its adaptation to the seriousness of the act constituting the infringement must be observed. The graduation of the sanction will especially consider the following criteria:
    a. The degree of guilt or the existence of intent.
    b. The continuity or persistence in the offending conduct.
    c. The nature of the damages caused.
    d. The recidivism, by commission in the term of one year, of more than one infraction of the same nature when this has been declared by a firm resolution in administrative proceedings.
4. When justified by the due adequacy between the sanction to be applied with the seriousness of the fact constituting the offense and the concurrent circumstances, the competent body to resolve it may impose the sanction in the lower degree.
5. When the commission of one offense necessarily results in the commission of another or others, only the sanction corresponding to the most serious offense committed must be imposed.
6. It will be punishable, as a continuous infringement, the realisation of a plurality of actions or omissions that infringe the same or similar administrative precepts, in execution of a preconceived plan or taking advantage of the same occasion."

In the Netherlands, special laws have a big variety of regulations on recidivism at the imposition of administrative penalties. A provision in the general regulation of administrative pecuniary sanctions is needed, but still lacking. Three examples clarifying the diversity are the regulation in the Act on the regulation of financial services (Wet op het financieel toezicht), the Act on Tobacco and smoking products (Tabaks- en rookwarenwet) and the Act on working hours (Arbeidstijdenwet).

"Article 1:81, fourth paragraph, **Act on the regulation of financial services** (Wet op het financieel toezicht)

If, at the time of the commission of the violation, five years have not elapsed since the imposition of an administrative pecuniary sanction on the violator for the same violation, the administrative pecuniary sanction for an individual violation shall not exceed twice the amount applicable pursuant to the second or third paragraph. maximum amount"

"Act on Tobacco and smoking products

Violations belonging to category B are punished with an administrative pecuniary sanction of EUR 45 000. This amount is increased to:

- EUR 135 000 if the natural person or legal entity to whom the violation can be attributed has previously been pecuniary sanctioned for a similar violation and two years have not passed since the previous administrative pecuniary sanction became irrevocable;
- EUR 225 000 if a similar violation is committed for the third time within three years after the administrative pecuniary sanction for the first violation has become irrevocable; and
- EUR 450 000 if a similar violation is committed for the fourth time within five years after the administrative pecuniary sanction for the first violation has become irrevocable."

"Article 10:7 Act on working hours

1. The administrative pecuniary sanction that can be imposed for a violation does not exceed the amount of the fifth category, referred to in Article 23, fourth paragraph, of the Criminal Code.
2. Without prejudice to the first paragraph, the official designated on the basis of Article 10:5, first or second paragraph, will increase the administrative pecuniary sanction to be imposed by 100% of the amount of the pecuniary sanction, determined on the basis of the sixth paragraph, if within a period of five years prior on the day of the discovery of the violation a previous violation, consisting of non-compliance with the same legal obligation or prohibition or non-compliance with similar obligations and prohibitions to be designated by or pursuant to an order in council, has been established and the administrative pecuniary sanction for the previous violation has become irrevocable.
3. The increase of the administrative pecuniary sanction referred to in the second paragraph is 200% if both the violation and the previous violation referred to in that paragraph have been designated as serious violations by or pursuant to an order in council.
4. Without prejudice to the first paragraph, the civil servant designated on the basis of Article 10:5, first or second paragraph, will increase the administrative pecuniary sanction to be imposed by 200% of the amount of the pecuniary sanction, determined on the basis of the sixth paragraph, if within a period of five years prior on the day of the discovery of the violation, twice a previous violation, consisting of non-compliance with the same legal obligation or prohibition or non-compliance with similar obligations and prohibitions to be designated by or pursuant to order in council, has been established and the administrative pecuniary sanctions for the previous violations have become irrevocable.
5. Notwithstanding the second and fourth paragraphs, the period of five years in those paragraphs is ten years if the irrevocable pecuniary sanctions referred to in those paragraphs have been imposed for serious violations designated by or pursuant to an order in council."

Source: OECD Research.

3.9. Bulgaria could provide for the deduction from the sanction of the time during which the sentenced person has been deprived administratively or de facto of the right to practise a particular profession or activity

The amendments to the AVPA of 2020 introduced in the administrative penalty legislation that "the time, during which for the same violation the punished person has been deprived by administrative procedure, or in fact of the opportunity to exercise a certain profession, or activity shall be deducted upon execution of the punishment temporary deprivation of the right to practice a certain profession or activity." (Article 29(a) of the AVPA)

The Institute referred to in Article 29a AVPA can therefore be applied in three situations:

- if the person has been deprived of the opportunity to pursue a particular profession or activity, in fact or by administrative procedure, in the course of the administrative proceedings initiated, which resulted in the issuance of a penalty order or the conclusion of an agreement, or by the imposition of an administrative penalty by the court in accordance with Article 58b of the AVPA for the offence in respect of which the person has been restricted;
- if the person has been deprived of the possibility of exercising a particular profession or activity, in fact or by administrative means, or in accordance with Article 69a of the Criminal Procedure Code, in the course of criminal proceedings on the basis of which administrative proceedings have been initiated, in accordance with Article 36 (2) of the AVPA;
- if the person has been deprived of the opportunity to pursue a particular profession or activity, in fact, either administratively or in accordance with Article 69a of the Criminal procedure Code, in the course of criminal proceedings, which result in the imposition of an administrative penalty on the defendant by the court, in accordance with Article 301 par.4 of the Criminal Procedure Code.

This Article is aimed at raising the standards regarding the right to protect citizens in administrative penalty proceedings and, in particular, at preventing the possibility for the convicted person to suffer restrictions of his rights for a period longer than that of the sentence imposed on him under Article 13, para. 1 (c) of the AVPA.

However, the AVPA does not have the legal possibility of deducting the period during which the offender is deprived, in fact or administratively, of the right to pursue a particular profession or activity, from the time when the penalty referred to in Article 13 para.1 (c) of the AVPA. Such a possibility is provided for in Article 59 (4) of the Criminal Code, but it refers to the crimes. This creates grounds for unjustifiably prolonged limitation of the offender's rights, unless the sanctioning authority applies the law by analogy, although this is generally not permissible in the administrative penalty law.

For example, a natural person who has committed a road traffic offence may be subject to a coercive administrative measure under Article 171 para.1 (b) of the Road Traffic Act — 'suspension of driving licences until the liability matter is being discussed, which is not a punishment, but cohesive measure in nature. At the same time, the penal decree may also impose on this person a penalty of disqualification from the right to drive, the execution of which begins on the date of entry into force of the penalty decree. In this way, the person penalised will be successively deprived of the possibility of driving a motor vehicle under the administrative coercive measure, for a period of up to six months and then also by virtue of the final penal decree.

In this regard, it is appropriate to provide for the possibility of deducting the time during which the sentenced person has been deprived administratively or de facto of the right to practise a particular profession or activity in other administrative criminal proceedings, as this is provided for the time during which the convicted person has been detained or placed under house arrest on charges of another offense on which the proceedings have been terminated or ended with an acquittal (see article 59, paragraph 3 of the Penal Code).

Such a solution is also appropriate if a person has been deprived, in fact or by reason of a coercive administrative measure, of the possibility of pursuing a particular profession or activity for a period exceeding the length of time for which the administrative penalty is to be served. The provision could be worded as proposed in (Box 3.6).

Box 3.6. Proposed Article 29a

"Article 29a. (new — SG Issue No. 109/2020, in force as of 23.12.2021)

(1) Time during which the person liable for the same offence has been administratively or de facto deprived of the possibility of exercising a particular profession or activity shall be deducted in the execution of the penalty of temporary disqualification from practising a definite profession or activity.

(2) The period during which, for the same offence, the person concerned has been deprived, by administrative or de facto, of the opportunity to pursue a particular profession or activity shall be deducted, in the event of execution of the punishment of temporary exclusion from the right to practice a particular profession or activity, imposed for another administrative offence of the same legislative act, where:

1. the administrative penalty proceedings for the offence for which the person has been administratively or de facto deprived of the opportunity to practice a particular profession or activity has resulted in a warning or resolution;
2. the length of time during which, for the same offence, the person liable has been administratively or de facto deprived of the opportunity to practice a particular profession or activity in excess of the duration of the penalty of suspension of the right to practice a particular profession or activity and, after the deduction referred to in paragraph 1 there is a remainder to be deducted."

Note: The text of para. 1 repeat art. 29a of AVPA - new, SG, iss. 109 of 2020, in force since 23.12.2021. Para. 2 is a new proposal.

Two additional issues do not find a clear solution in the law. Firstly when, despite the conditions for doing so, the sanctioning authority or the court fails to gather evidence of whether the rights of the infringer have been limited in the sense discussed above or fail to apply the institute referred to in Article 29a of the AVPA. The sanctioning authority could not issue an additional penalty order, because according to Interpretative Decision of the General Assembly of Penal Chamber of the Supreme Court of Cassation of 17.06.1986 in Case No 75/1985 the sanctioning authority could decide only on the assets which were to be confiscated for the benefit of the State and the disposal of the material evidence if it had failed to make a decision in its final law enforcement order. Secondly, in case when, at the date of the final enforcement order by the sanctioning authority, the order imposing the coercive administrative measure by virtue of which the infringer is restricted in his rights has been appealed and has not entered into force.

These two issues should be recommended to make explicit provision in the law. In the first place, it is possible that the additional penal order is expressly laid down by law (Box 3.7).

Box 3.7. Proposed Article 58(4) of the AVPA

"Article 58 (4) The sanctioning authority may issue an additional penalty order on the matters referred to in Article 57 par.1, item 9 to 11 if it has failed to do so by means of the penal order."

Note: New provision proposed by the OECD.

Secondly, it is possible to introduce a provision relating to the execution of administrative penalties (Box 3.8).

Box 3.8. Proposed Article 81(3) of the AVPA

"**Article 81.** (3). Where Article 29a is not applied by the sanctioning authority or by the court, it shall be applied by the authority referred to in paragraph 1."

Note: New provision proposed by the OECD.

References

Council of Europe (2020), *Liability of Legal Persons for Corruption Offences*, https://rm.coe.int/liability-of-legal-persons/16809ef7a0 (accessed on 25 June 2021). [4]

European Committee on Crime Problems (2020), *Replies to Questionnaire on Administrative Sanctions*, https://rm.coe.int/cdpc-2019-1-replies-to-questionnaire-on-administrative-sanctions/168093669b (accessed on 24 June 2021). [1]

OECD (2021), *Implementing the OECD Anti-Bribery Convention. Phase 4 Report: Bulgaria*, OECD, Paris, https://www.oecd.org/corruption/bulgaria-oecdanti-briberyconvention.htm (accessed on 27 October 2021). [2]

OECD (2016), *The Liability of Legal Persons for Foreign Bribery: A Stocktaking Report*, OECD, Paris, https://www.oecd.org/daf/anti-bribery/Liability-Legal-Persons-Foreign-Bribery-Stocktaking.pdf (accessed on 24 June 2021). [3]

4 Administrative penalty proceedings in Bulgaria

This last chapter analyses procedural issues of administrative penalty law. It deals with principles, rights and standards applicable to and during proceedings, rules to serve summons and notices as well as to possible procedural dynamics such as suspension, consolidation and in absentia proceedings. Recommendations and proposals build on the draft Code of Administrative Violations and Penalties of 2015, whose proposals represent a valuable basis to complement the legal framework and avoid gaps and loopholes that emerged in practice.

4.1. The AVPA could provide for more detailed and extensive rules for proving administrative violations and the identity of the offender

The AVPA does not contain rules for proving the administrative violation and the identity of the offender. The only rules for proving the administrative violations are those for the seizure of material evidence by the act for establishing an administrative violation. The rules of the Criminal Procedure Code apply by virtue of the restrictive reference contained in Article 84 of AVPA. However, these rules do not apply in the out-of-court phase of the proceedings and regulate the proof of the crime, which is why they presuppose significant formalism. The need to ensure the availability of the full range of investigative tools of the Criminal Procedure Code, including special intelligence means, in proceedings against legal persons was also underscored by the OECD Working Group on Bribery in relation to foreign bribery investigations (OECD, 2021[1]).

The AVPA could explicitly provide that the rules of the Code of Criminal Procedure apply accordingly in relation to the proof of offences, by laying down exceptions to these rules. Such exceptions are for example the involvement of witnesses of the procedural actions, for judicial review of measures of inquiry, etc. However, future codification could provide the detailed rules on proof in administrative criminal proceedings.

A good basis for concrete legislative proposals can be found in the draft Code of Administrative Violations and Penalties of 2015. Taking that text as basis, the specific wording of the provisions in the codification act could be as proposed in Box 4.1.

Box 4.1 Proposed procedural rules for administrative penalty proceedings

"CHAPTER...

EVIDENCING

Section I. GENERAL PROVISIONS

Subject to evidencing

Article 1.

(1) In administrative criminal proceedings, the following shall be proved:

1. the violation committed;
2. the participation in the commitment of the offence of the person against whom the act for establishment of the administrative violation has been drawn up;
3. the circumstances relevant to the liability of the person against whom the act for establishment of the administrative violation has been drawn up.

(2) The provisions of this chapter shall be applicable also for the circumstances relevant to the liability of the sole trader or legal entity for failure to fulfil an obligation towards the State or municipality in the course of their activities.

Burden of proof

Article 2.

(1) The burden of proving the violation shall fall onto the sanctioning authority.

(2) The person against whom the act for establishment of the administrative violation has been drawn up is not required to prove that he has not committed the infringement.

(3) No conclusions can be drawn to the detriment of the person against whom the act for establishment of the administrative violation has been drawn up in case he has not given or refuses to provide explanations or has failed to substantiate his objections.

(4) Paragraphs 2 and 3 shall apply mutatis mutandis to the sole trader and to the legal person entity representing the legal entities against whom the administrative infringement notice has been drawn up.

Evidence and evidence means

Article 3.

(1) The evidence may be factual data relating to the circumstances of the administrative proceedings, which contribute to their clarification and are established in accordance with the procedure laid down in that code.

(2) The evidence means shall be used to reproduce evidence or other evidence means.

(3) Evidence and evidence means which has not been obtained or associated in accordance with the conditions and procedures laid down in this Code shall not be admissible.

Methods of evidencing

Article 4. Evidence in administrative criminal proceedings shall be carried out using the methods provided for in this Code.

Collection of evidence

Article 5.

(1) The act issuer, the sanctioning authority and the court shall collect evidence ex- officio or at the request of the persons concerned.

(2) The act issuer, the sanctioning authority and the court collect and verify both evidence supporting the findings of the offence and aggravating the liability of the person against whom the administrative offence has been issued and evidence exculpating or mitigating liability.

(3) Paragraph 2 shall also apply mutatis mutandis to the taking of evidence of the liability of the sole trader or legal entity against whom the act of the establishment of the administrative violation has been drawn up.

(4) The collection of evidence cannot be refused on the sole ground that the request was not made within a certain time limit.

Actions by delegation

Article 6.

(1) Acts of collecting the evidence by delegation shall be permitted where they are to be carried out outside the area of the authority dealing with the case or file and their performance by that authority presents particular difficulties.

(2) Where it is ordered by a court, the delegation is executed by a judge of the district court concerned and, where ordered by the act issuer or sanctioning authority, by the relevant authority.

(3) Where it considers it necessary, the authority dealing with the case or the file may carry out individual actions under paragraph 1 also in the area of another authority.

Section II. EVIDENCE AND EVIDENCE MEANS

Types of evidence

Article 7. The evidence shall be material and written.

Material evidence

Article 8.

(1) As material evidence shall be collected and checked the objects intended or used to commit the violation, which are traceable to the violation or have been the object of the violation, as well as any other objects which may serve to clarify the circumstances of the proceedings.

(2) The material evidence shall be attached to the case file, taking care not to damage or modify or, if that is not possible, described in an appropriate record and, if possible, photographed.

(3) When the case file is passed from one body to another, the material evidence shall be delivered together with it.

(4) Material evidence, which because of their dimensions or for other reasons cannot be attached to the file, must, where possible, be sealed and stored in the places specified by the respective authority.

(5) Cash and other valuables shall be transferred for safekeeping to a commercial bank serving the state budget or to the Bulgarian National Bank.

Safe-keeping of material evidence

Article 9.

(1) The material evidence shall be kept until the administrative criminal proceedings have been completed. Seized items shall be handed over for safe-keeping in accordance with the rules laid down. In the absence of such rules, the items shall be handed over to the department of the act issuer. Where appropriate, they may be handed over for preservation of the offender or other persons.

(2) Objects seized as material evidence, the possession of which is prohibited, shall be delivered to the relevant authorities or shall be destroyed.

Written evidence

Article 10.

(1) Documents which contribute to the clarification of the circumstances referred to in Article 1 shall be collected and checked as documentary evidence.

(2) A certified copy or excerpt of a document shall have the same evidentiary value as the original. Upon request, any person shall be obliged to produce the document in its original form.

(3) The electronic document may be presented on paper in the form of a certified copy. Upon request, any person shall be required to present the document in digital form.

(4) Documents submitted in a foreign language shall be accompanied by an accurate translation into Bulgarian.

Disposal of material and written evidence

Article 11.

(1) Except as provided for in Article (20-21 AVPA), objects seized as material evidence shall be confiscated for the benefit of the State where:

1. it has not been established who they belong to and they have not been sought within one year of the conclusion of the administrative criminal proceedings;
2. the person to whom they belong to is identified, the person entitled has been duly informed to appear in order the objects to be returned and they have not been sought within six months of the notification.

(2) Objects seized as material evidence may, with the permission of the sanctioning authority, be returned to those who are entitled before the conclusion of the administrative criminal proceedings, where this will not hinder the disclosure of the objective truth and are not subject to forfeiture in favour of the State.

(3) The refusal of the sanctioning authority under paragraph 2 shall not be open to an appeal.

(4) The goods subject to rapid dissolution could be sold, with the permission of the sanctioning authority, through state and municipal companies, and the amount received, after deduction of the costs incurred, is deposited with a commercial bank servicing the state budget or with the Bulgarian National Bank.

(5) At the end of the administrative criminal proceedings, books or other written documents collected as material or written evidence shall be placed in the case file or handed over to the institutions, legal entities and natural persons concerned. Objects seized as material evidence, the possession of which is prohibited, shall be delivered to the relevant establishments or be destroyed.

(6) Where a dispute arises over a right over objects collected as material evidence to be decided by a court, they are kept until the court's decision becomes final. The final decision of the court is binding on the sanctioning authority in matters of civil status and property rights.

Types of evidence means

Article 12. Evidence shall be established by vocal, material and written evidence means.

Verbal evidence means

Article 13. Verbal evidence means are:

1. the explanations of the person against whom the act of the establishment of the administrative violation has been drawn up;
2. witness statements.

Explanations

Article 14.

(1) The person against whom the act of the establishment of the administrative violation has been drawn up shall have the right to give or refuse to give explanations to the inspection body, the act issuer, the sanctioning authority or the court.

(2) The penal order cannot be based solely on the confession of the person against whom the act of the establishment of the administrative violation has been drawn up;

(3) The confession of the person against whom the act of the establishment of the administrative violation has been drawn up does not relieve the authorities concerned of their obligation to collect further evidence.

Persons who cannot be witnesses

Article 15.

(1) A person who has participated in the same proceedings in different procedural capacity cannot be a witness unless:

1. the person against whom the administrative criminal proceedings has been terminated;
2. the inspection body;
3. the act issuer.

(2) a person who, because of physical or psychological disabilities, is not capable of correctly perceiving the facts relevant to the proceedings or to give credible testimony to them cannot be a witness.

Persons who may refuse to testify

Article 16. May refuse to testify:

1. the spouse, ascendants, descendants, siblings of the person against whom the act of the establishment of the administrative violation has been drawn up and the person with whom he/she is in coexistence;
2. the sole trader against whom the act of the establishment of the administrative violation has been drawn up;
3. representing and managing the sole trader, the legal entity against whom the administrative violation has been drawn up.

Witness testimonies

Article 17. Testimony may establish all the facts which the witness has accepted and which contribute to revealing the objective truth.

Rights and obligations of the witness

Article 18.

(1) The witness shall have the right to:

1. use notes of figures, dates, etc. in his possession relating to his testimonies;
2. receive the expenses he has made;
3. requires the annulment of acts which adversely affect his rights and legitimate interests.

(2) A witness shall have the right to consult a lawyer if they consider that the answer to the question referred affects his rights under Article 14 (1). Upon request, the act issuer, the sanctioning authority or the court shall provide for this possibility

(3) The witness has the obligation to:

1. appears before the relevant authority when summoned;
2. sets out everything he knows about the circumstances of the proceedings;
3. answers the questions he is asked

(4) A witness who is unable to appear because of illness or disability may be questioned where he or she is present.

Circumstances, in which the witness shall not be obliged to testify

Article 19.

(1) The witness is not obliged to testify on questions the answers to which would accuse him/her or his/her ascendants, descendants, brothers or sisters or spouse, or the person with whom he/she is in a factual coexistence in the commission of a crime or other offence.

(2) The witness cannot be questioned on the circumstances which have been entrusted to him as a legal representative.

Written evidence means

Article 20.

(1) Written evidence means are:

1. the statements of findings;
2. the protocols of the collection of evidence;
3. the protocols for the establishment of material evidence means;
4. other documents.

(2) The protocol shall include:

1. the date and place of the action concerned;
2. the time when the action started and ended;
3. details of the persons who participated in the action carried out;
4. the actions carried out and their sequence;
5. evidence collected;
6. the requests, observations and objections made.

(3) The record shall be signed by the authority which carried out the act in question and by other participants in administrative criminal proceedings in the cases provided for in this Code.

(4) All corrections, amendments and additions to the protocol shall be certified by the signature of the persons referred to in paragraph 3.

(5) Reports drawn up in accordance with the procedure laid down in this Code shall constitute evidence of the performance of the acts concerned, of the procedure in which they were carried out and of the evidence obtained.

Material evidence means

Article 21.

(1) Where material evidence cannot be separated from the place where it is found and in other cases provided for in this Code, the inspection body, the act issuer, the sanctioning body or the court shall produce photographs, slides, cinemas, videogames, phonograms, recordings on a computer data carrier, plans, diagrams, memoranda or prints.

(2) Computer data shall also be recorded on paper where necessary.

(3) Where special knowledge and qualification is required, a technical assistant shall be appointed.

(4), persons referred to in Article 15 (2) cannot be technical assistants.

(5) The technical assistant carries out the task assigned to him them under the direct supervision and direction of the authority which appointed him.

(6) The materials referred to in paragraph 1 shall be attached to the case file.

Obligation to preserve and transmit evidence

Article 22.

(1) At the request of the inspection body, the act issuer, the sanctioning authority or the court, all institutions, legal entities, officials and citizens shall retain and transmit the objects, papers and computer data in their possession which may be relevant for administrative penalty proceedings, unless special procedures are laid down for their collection.

(2) Where the collection of evidence is subject to a ruling by a court of law, jurisdiction lies with the court which, in accordance with the rules of that code, decides on an appeal against the penalty order.

Section III. METHODS OF EVIDENCING

Types of methods of evidencing

Article 23.

(1) The methods of evidencing are the interrogation, expert examination, inspection, search, seizure, inquisitorial experiment, recognition of persons and objects.

(2) Where necessary, the examination, search, seizure and inquisitorial experiment shall be carried out in the presence of an expert or of a specialist technical assistant. The persons referred to in Article 15 par.2 cannot be technical assistants. The technical assistant carries out the task assigned to him under the direct supervision and direction of the authority which appointed him.

(3) In the application of the procedures referred to in paragraph 1, the provisions of the relevant special laws shall apply to lawyers, notaries or private bailiffs.

Interrogation of the person against whom the act for the establishment of the administrative violation has been drawn up

Article 24.

(1) The interrogation of the person against whom the act for the establishment of the administrative violation has been drawn up shall take place during the day, unless it is urgent.

(2) Prior to the hearing, the authority carrying out the interrogation shall establish the identity of the person.

(3) The interrogation of the person against whom the act for the establishment of the administrative violation has been drawn up begins by asking whether he understands what offence he is accused of, and then invited to disclose, if he so wishes, in a form of free narrative, everything he knows about the circumstances to be proved.

(4) Questions may be put to the person against whom the act for the establishment of the administrative violation has been drawn up to supplement his explanations or to remedy incompleteness, ambiguity or contradictions.

(5) The questions must be clear, concrete and related to the circumstances of the proceedings. They should not suggest answers or lead to a particular answer.

(6) Where the act for the establishment of the administrative violation is drawn up against two or more persons, they shall be interrogated separately.

(7) Where the person against whom the act for the establishment of the administrative violation is drawn up wishes and will not have the effect of postponing the measure of taking evidence, his interrogation shall be carried out in the presence of his legal representative.

(8) The interrogation of the person against whom the act for the establishment of the administrative violation has been drawn up may also be conducted via videoconference or teleconference, for which electronic and paper records are drawn up and attached to the case.

(9) In the cases referred to in paragraph 8, the identification of the witness shall be carried out by an authority referred to in Article 87 (2) or by a police authority.

Interrogation of a witness

Article 25.

(1) The interrogation of a witness shall take place during the day, unless it is urgent.

(2) Prior the interrogation, the identity of the witness and his or her relations with the other participants in the proceedings shall be established.

(3) The authority conducting the interrogation shall invite the witness to testify in good faith and shall warn him/her of the responsibility before the law in case he/she refuses to give testimony, or neglects certain circumstances.

(4) The witness shall make a promise that he/she will state in good faith and precisely everything he/she knows in connection with the case.

(5) The right to refuse to testify shall be explained to the persons referred to in Articles 97 and 100.

(6) The witness shall state, in a free narrative form, everything he/she is aware of regarding the case.

(7) A minor witness shall be interviewed in the presence of a pedagogue or psychologist and, where necessary, in the presence of his/her parent or legal guardian. The authority conducting the hearing shall explain to the minor witness the need to give a testimony without warning him of liability.

(8) A minor witness shall be interrogated in the presence of the persons under the para. 7, if the respective body deems so necessary.

(9) The interrogation of the witness may also be carried out via videoconference or teleconference, for which a record is drawn up in electronic and paper form which are attached to the case.

(10) In the cases referred to in paragraph 9, the identification of the witness shall be carried out by an authority referred to in Article 87 (2) or by a police authority.

Interrogation by delegation

Article 26.

(1) The person against whom the act for establishment of the administrative violation has been drawn up or witness may be interrogated by delegation if it has to be committed outside the jurisdiction of the act issuer, the sanctioning authority or the court and there are particular difficulties in their being committed by that authority.

(2) Where it is ordered by a court, the delegation is carried out by a judge of the district court concerned and, where it is ordered by an act issuer or a sanctioning authority, by a relevant act issuer or sanctioning authority.

Interrogating with an interpreter and Interpreter in Bulgarian sign language

Article 27.

(1) Detailed with the participation of an interpreter or interpreter shall take place in the cases referred to in Article....

(2) A person referred to in Article 15 (2) may not be an interpreter or interpreter.

Cross-examination

Article 28.

(1) A cross- examination may be made in the event of a significant contradiction between:

1. the explanations of the persons against whom the act has been drawn up;
2. the explanations of the persons referred to in subparagraph 1 and the testimonies of witnesses;
3. testimony.

(2) Before questioning, the persons between whom a cross- examination is made are asked whether or not they know each other and what their relationship is.

(3) With the permission of the relevant authority, persons taking part in cross- examination may ask each other questions.

Expert's examination

Article 29.

(1) Where special knowledge in the field of science, art or technology is required in order to clarify certain circumstances of the case, the act issuer, the sanctioning authority or the court shall order an expert's examination.

(2) The expert 's examination shall be mandatory where there is doubt about:

1. the sanity of the person against whom the act for establishment of the administrative violation has been drawn up;
2. the ability of the person against whom the act for establishment of the administrative violation has been drawn up, having regard to his physical and mental state, to correctly perceive the facts relevant to the subject matter of the evidence and to give plausible explanations of them;
3. the capacity of the witness, having regard to his physical and mental condition, to correctly perceive the facts relevant to the subject matter of the evidence and to give credible testimony to them.

(3) The act instituting an expert examination shall specify: the grounds which necessitate the performance of the examination; the object and the task of the expert examination; the materials presented to the expert; the expert's full name, education, specialty, scientific degree and official position or the name of the establishment, where the expert works, the name of the medical establishment, where the stationary observations will be performed and the term of presentation of the opinion.

(4) The authority which appoints the expert's examination may require the person against whom the act for establishment of the administrative violation has been drawn up; from the sole trader or the representative of the citizens' organisation against whom the act for establishment of the administrative violation has been drawn up; from the witness samples for comparative examination, where it is not possible to obtain them in any other way.

(5) The persons referred to in paragraph 4 shall be obliged to provide the required samples for comparative examination and, if they are refused, they shall be forcibly seized with the permission of a judge of the district court, who shall be competent to rule on an appeal or a prosecutor's protest against the penal order.

Persons to whom an expert examination is to be entrusted

Article 30.

(1) An expert examination shall be entrusted to experts from the appropriate field of the science, art or techniques.

(2) Persons, who shall not be experts:

1. the persons against whom the grounds referred to in Article....apply ;
2. witnesses on the case;
3. persons who are ex officio or otherwise dependent on the person against whom the act for establishment of the administrative violation has been drawn up or his/her legal representative;
4. persons who are employees or are associated with the sole trader or the legal entity against whom act for establishment of the administrative violation has been drawn up or their legal representative;
5. the persons who carried out the inspection, the materials of which served as a basis for initiating the proceedings;
6. persons who do not possess the necessary professional qualifications.

(3) In the cases referred to in paragraph (2), the experts shall be obliged to challenge themselves.

(4) Where the expert fails to comply with the obligation referred to in paragraph 3, the expert shall be removed by the act issuer, the sanctioning authority or the court of its own motion or at the request of the person concerned. The person concerned shall bring an action before the authority which ordered the expert's examination.

Service of the document appointing an expert's examination

Article 31.

(1) The authority which appointed the expert shall call upon the expert, check identity, education and qualifications, and whether there are any grounds for objection.

(2) The decision commissioning an expert assessment shall be served on the expert witness, who shall then be informed of their rights and obligations and of their liability if they submit false conclusions.

Rights and obligations of the expert

Article 32.

(1) The expert is entitled to:

1. acquaint himself with the materials of the procedure relating to the expert's examination;
2. request additional material and participate in individual evidence-gathering activities where this is necessary in order to fulfil the task assigned to it;
3. is remunerated for the work performed;
4. shall be paid for the expenses he has incurred;
5. requires the annulment of acts which adversely affect rights and legitimate interests.

(2) Where there are two or more experts, they shall be entitled to consult one another before they give an opinion. In case of consensus, the experts may assign one of them to expose the general opinion before the respective body, and where there is a difference in opinions, each of them shall present a separate opinion.

(3) The expert shall be obliged to appear before the relevant authority when summonsed and to submit conclusions on the questions of the examination.

(4) A court hearing of an expert outside the country may also take place via videoconference or telephone conference where the circumstances of the case so require.

Expert's opinion

Article 33.

(1) After carrying out the necessary examinations, the expert shall draw a written conclusion, in which he/she shall state:

1. his/ her name and the grounds on which the expert examination was carried out;
2. where the expert's examination was carried out;
3. the task that has been assigned;
4. the materials which have been used;
5. the examination carried out and by which scientific and technical means;
6. the results obtained;
7. the conclusions of the expert examination.

(2) The statement shall be signed by the expert and, where more than one expert is appointed, by each of them.

(3) Where the expert's examination reveals new material which is relevant to the proceedings but in respect of which no task has been assigned to, the expert shall be required to mention them in his report.

(4) The expert opinion is not mandatory for the act issuer, the sanctioning authority and the court.

(5) Where an authority disagrees with the conclusion of an expert, it shall be obliged to state its reasons.

Additional and repeat expert examination

Article 34.

(1) An additional expert examination shall be appointed when the expert's examination is not sufficiently completed and clear.

(2) A repeat expert examination shall be appointed where the expert's statement is not well grounded and a doubt about its correctness arises.

Inspection

Article 35.

(1) The control body, the act issuer, the sanctioning authority or the court may inspect locations, premises or objects in order to discover, investigate and preserve traces of the offence or other evidence necessary to clarify the circumstances of the administrative criminal proceedings.

(2) The inspection shall be carried out during the day, unless it is urgent

(3) Upon performing the inspection everything shall be examined as it has been found and after that the necessary movements shall be made.

Searches and seizures

Article 36.

(1) Where there is sufficient reason to believe that objects, papers or computer information systems containing information data which may be relevant to the proceedings are located in any premises or person, a search shall be carried out to detect and seize them.

(2) The search and seizure shall be carried out in the presence of the person using the premises or an adult member of his or her family. Where the user of the premises or a member of their family cannot be present, search and seizure shall be performed in the presence of the house manager or a representative of the municipality or mayor's office.

(3) Search and seizure on premises used by state or municipal services shall be conducted in the presence of a representative of the office.

(4) Searches and seizures in premises used by a sole trader or a legal entity shall be carried out in the presence of their representative. Where a representative of the sole trader or the organisation of citizens cannot be present, the search and seizure shall be carried out in the presence of a representative of the municipality or town hall.

(5) Searches and seizures at the premises of foreign representations of international organisations and in the accommodation of their officials who enjoy immunity from the administrative criminal jurisdiction of the Republic of Bulgaria shall be carried out with the consent of the Head of Representation and in the presence of a representative of the Ministry of Foreign Affairs.

(6) Searches and seizures concerning computer information systems and software applications shall be conducted in the presence of an expert technical assistant.

(7) Search and seizure shall be conducted during the daytime, unless they can be delayed. Before carrying out a search and seizure, the relevant authority shall propose to indicate to it the objects, papers or computer information systems sought containing computer information data.

(8) When conducting search and seizure, no actions shall be undertaken unless they are necessary for the purposes thereof. Premises and storerooms shall be forced open only in the event of a refusal to open them and unnecessary damages must be avoided.

(9) Where the search and seizure reveal circumstances related to the private life of citizens, the necessary measures not to disclose them shall be taken.

(10) The seized objects, papers and computer information systems containing computer data shall be handled to those present. Where necessary, they shall be bagged and sealed at the place where they were seized.

(11) Where carried out by an act issuer or a sanctioning authority, search and seizure shall be carried out with the permission of a judge of the district court who is competent to rule on an appeal or appeal against the penalty order.

(12) In urgent cases, where this is the only possibility of gathering and preserving evidence, the act issuer and the sanctioning authority may carry out a search and seizure without the authorisation referred to in paragraph 11, and the record of the taking of evidence carried out shall be submitted to the judge for approval without delay and no later than 24 hours.

(13) In judicial proceedings, search and seizure are carried out by decision of the court hearing the case.

Search of a person

Article 37.

(1) The search of a person shall be permitted where there is sufficient reason to believe that the person has concealed objects or documents relevant to the administrative criminal proceedings.

(2) The search shall be carried out by a person of the same sex.

(3) In the case of searches, Article 36 (6) to (14) shall apply accordingly.

Investigation experiment

Article 38.

(1) The act issuer, the sanctioning authority or the court may carry out an investigation experiment in order to verify and specify data obtained from the questioning of the witness or the person against whom the act for establishment of the administrative violation has been drawn up, or from any other measure of inquiry.

(2) The investigation experiment shall be permitted provided that the dignity of the persons participating in the experiment is not stripped of and that there is no danger to their health.

Recognition

Article 39.

(1) Recognition of persons or objects shall be carried out when it is necessary to confirm the identity of persons and objects in order to clarify the circumstances of the proceedings.

(2) The act issuer, the sanctioning authority or the court shall propose to the person against whom the act for establishment of the administrative violation has been drawn up or to the witness to identify a person or object.

(3) Immediately before recognition is carried out, the person is questioned whether he knows the person or object to be recognised; the characteristics on which he can recognise them; the circumstances in which he/she observed the person or object; and the condition in which he/she was perceived by the person or object to be identified.

(4) A person shall be presented for identification together with three or more persons similar in appearance to that person and measures shall be taken to avoid direct contact between that person and the identifying person.

(5) At the discretion of the authority performing the recognition, it may be carried out in such a way that the person identifying the person does not appear directly with the identified person.

(6) An object shall be presented for identification together with three or more homogeneous objects.

(7) Where it is not possible to show the person or object themselves, a photograph shall be displayed together with the photographs of three or more persons similar in appearance or photographs of three or more homogeneous objects.

(8) Where several persons referred to in paragraph (2) are required to recognise persons or objects, they shall be shown separately on each of the identifiable persons, ensuring that the identification persons do not come into direct contact with each other. Simultaneous identification by several individuals shall be inadmissible.

(9) The person referred to in paragraph (2) shall be proposed, by specifying the person or object to which the statements or statements given by him or her relate, to explain how they have recognised them.

(10) Photo album may be used for recognition."

Note: The texts basically reproduce the provisions of the 2015 draft of the Administrative Violation Code (Art. 82 - Art. 121). The proposed wording is in compliance with the concepts and definition of the current AVPA in relation to sole traders and legal entities. Numbering starts from one for indicative purposes only.

With regards to the related issue of the ascertainment of the offender´s identity, the curret wording of Article 43 of the AVPA provides that "when the identity of the offender cannot be established by the issuer of the act it shall be established by the closest municipal administration or division of the Ministry of Interior." According to the interviews carried out within the fact-finding mission with key ministries and agencies making use of the administrative penalty framework, this text creates practical difficulties because it requires the intervention of the Ministry of Interior´s officials each time there are problems in establishing the identity of the offender. To overcome this challenge and swift the process of ascertaining the offender´s identity, Bulgaria could amend the relevant text by giving the right to require a personal document to any official issuing an act for establishment of the committed administrative violation along the proposal illustrated in Box 4.2.

Box 4.2. Proposed art. 43 (3) of AVPA

"**Art. 43.** (3) In order to establish the identity of the offender, the act issuer shall have the right to require an identity document or another document in lieu thereof. Where the offender does not present identity document or it is not possible to establish his identity from the document presented, it shall be established by the nearest municipal administration or department of the Ministry of the Interior."

Source: OECD based on a proposal brought up during fact-finding interviews.

4.1.1. Revising the regulation on seizure of material evidence

For the purposes of the administrative penalty proceedings, when establishing administrative violations the issuer of the act can seize and keep the material evidence related to the establishment of the offence, as well as the objects subject to seizure in favour of the state (Article 41 of the AVPA). This requires that they are being described in the act establishing the administrative violation.

In these proceedings, unlike in the criminal proceedings, there is no need for judicial approval of the actions of the organ seizing the property, although searches and related seizures significantly restrict the legal sphere of the person subject to that investigative measure. Furthermore, the law does not explicitly regulate the possibility for seizing and attaching the material evidence after drawing up the act and during the proceedings.

Another issue concerns the safekeeping and disposal of the material evidence contained in the file until the case is solved. The procedural administrative penalty law is extremely laconic on this issue. For example, there are no rules as to whether the seized material evidence should be kept until the end of the administrative criminal proceedings, neither are there rules as to whether it is permissible to dispose of these items outside the hypothesis of Article 46, paragraph 4 AVPA, before the end of the proceedings before the sanctioning body. The law does not contain any reference to the Criminal Procedure Code on these issues either.

At the same time, the seized items may include ones that are important for the offender or items of value significantly exceeding even the maximum amount of the proprietary sanction provided for the violation. It is also possible that the items are not relevant to the subject of proof, but the administrative authority nevertheless wrongfully refuses to return them to the person against whom the act has been drawn up.

In the absence of explicit regulation, the possible conclusion is that the matter is left to the discretion of the sanctioning authority. This circumstance hides a serious risk of unjustified return of items attached as material evidence or means of proof to an entitled or non-entitled person. There is also a risk of unjustified detention of items that are not relevant to the proceedings (not a source of relevant facts) in order to motivate the entitled person to dispose of the service intended by the administrative body. Additionally, it may lead to corrupt administrative practices.

This legal gap could be addressed by creating a more robust gal framework regulating the power of the sanctioning body to dispose of items seized in the file before the end of the proceedings and preventing the sanctioning body from refusing to return the irrelevant items.

Proposals to regulate matters relating to the keeping and disposal of material and documentary evidence in a future codification act have already been referred to in Box 4.1. Under the current AVPA, the provisions could be worded as proposed in Box 4.3.

Box 4.3. Proposed Articles 41, 46 and 21a

"**Article 41** When administrative offences are found, the act issuer may seize material evidence relating to the establishment of the violation, as well as the items to be confiscated for the benefit of the State under Articles 20 and 21. The rules of the Code of Criminal Procedure shall apply to the procedure for seizing material evidence."

"**Article 46.**

(1) The seized items shall be kept until the administrative penalty proceedings have been completed. Seized items shall be handed over for safe-keeping in accordance with the rules laid down. In the absence of such rules, the items shall be handed over to the department of the collector. Where appropriate, they may be handed over for preservation by the offender or other persons.

(2) Objects seized as material evidence, the possession of which is prohibited, shall be delivered to the relevant establishments or be destroyed.

(3) Objects seized as material evidence may, with the permission of the sanctioning authority, be returned to those entitled before the conclusion of the administrative penalty proceedings, where this will not hinder the disclosure of the objective truth and are not subject to forfeiture in favour of the State.

(4) The refusal of the sanctioning authority under paragraph 3 shall not be appealed.

(5) The goods spoiling are sold, with the permission of the sanctioning authority, through state and municipal companies, and the amount received, after deduction of the costs incurred, is deposited with a commercial bank servicing the state budget or with the Bulgarian National Bank.

(6) At the end of the administrative penalty proceedings, books or other written documents collected as material or written evidence shall be placed in the case file or handed over to the institutions, legal entities and natural persons concerned. Objects seized as material evidence, the possession of which is prohibited, shall be delivered to the relevant establishments or be destroyed.

(7) Where a dispute arises over a right over objects collected as material evidence to be decided by a court, they are kept until the court's decision becomes final. The final decision of the court is binding on the sanctioning authority in matters of civil status and property rights."

"**Article 21a.** Except in the cases provided for in Articles 20 and 21, objects seized as material evidence shall be confiscated for the benefit of the State where:

1. it has not been established who they belong to and have not been sought within one year of the conclusion of the administrative criminal proceedings;
2. the person to whom they belong is found, the person entitled has been duly informed to appear in order for them to be returned and have not been sought within six months of the notification."

Note: This proposal is based on the draft Administrative Violations and Penalties Code of 2015 with some edits and additions.

4.2. The AVPA could introduce provisionson the separation and consolidation of proceedings

The procedural rules in the AVPA only regulate the case when the act establishing the administrative violation concerns for a single violation and this violation is the subject of the final law enforcement act issued by the sanctioning body. However, there are also cases when it is possible or even appropriate from the perspective of procedural economy that the act is drawn up for two or more violations. In these cases, it is not always possible to launch proceedings for both offences. For example, if the offences fall within the scope of competence of different enforcement authorities, it may be that one of the offences requires collecting of evidence or there are grounds for suspension of proceedings, etc., and for the second one it is not necessary. It is therefore appropriate to develop provisions for the separation of files in the procedural law. This could also be done within the court phase of the proceedings, but in such case, the rules of the Criminal Procedure Code will apply.

It is also possible that there is a connection between two or more administrative penalty files. In such case, it is appropriate to provide for the possibility of merging proceedings in the general administrative law. The provisions concerning the exercise of the powers of the sanctioning authority in this respect could be worded as proposed in Box 4.4.

Box 4.4. Proposed Articles on separation and consolidation of proceedings

"Proceedings separation

Article X.

(1) Where evidence of the involvement of more persons in the commission of the violation has been gathered, the sanctioning authority may separate the materials for some of them in separate proceedings where:

1. their treatment in a single proceeding would hinder the course of those proceedings;
2. some of the persons are not identified;
3. there is reason to stop the proceedings in respect of one or more of the persons.

(2) Where evidence of several violations involving the same person has been gathered, the sanctioning authority may separate the material for some of the violations where dealing with them in one proceeding would hinder the course of those proceedings.

(3) Where evidence of several violations involving the same person has been gathered and the sanctioning authority has jurisdiction to rule only in respect of some of them, it shall separate the material for the offences for which it does not have jurisdiction and shall forward it to the competent sanctioning authority."

"Consolidation of proceedings

Article X. Where it is established that two or more proceedings instituted for different violations or against different persons have a link with each other, the sanctioning authority may bring them together if this is necessary to reveal the objective truth and will not impede the course of the proceedings."

Note: This proposal is based on the draft Administrative Violations and Penalties Code of 2015 with some edits and additions.

It is also necessary to provide for the possibility of bringing together two or more administrative penal cases at the stage of judicial review of administrative acts, where there is an objective or subjective link between them, as it is possible with criminal cases. Such a need would arise, for example, when contesting:

- two or more acts of the sanctioning authority issued against two or more persons concerning their involvement, even in a different administrative-punitive capacity, in the commission of the same administrative offence (for example, as perpetrator and supporter, as perpetrator and as an admitter, in simultaneous sanctioning the legal person and the legal entity representing it, etc.);
- two or more acts of the sanctioning authority issued against the same person for two or more violations committed in the same factual context (e.g. two or more violation of the Road Traffic Act committed in the same time, place and circumstances, two or more infringements of the VAT Act in two consecutive tax periods, etc.);
- two or more acts of the sanctioning authority against the same person for the same violation, issued contrary to the principle *non bis in idem* (in order to ensure a lawful assessment of which of them should be annulled);
- main and additional penal orders.

Similarly, it would also be important to provide for the opposite possibility of splitting of proceedings, which would be needed when:

- the proceedings are initiated following an appeal or protest against a penal order sanctioning the offender for two or more offences committed in different judicial districts;
- the proceedings are initiated following an appeal or protest against a penal order sanctioning one or more persons for offences with no connection between them;
- the conditions for the stop of proceedings against one or more of the persons pecuniary sanctioned are met, and the other conditions are not met.

Box 4.5 proposes two articles on splitting and consolidation of cases.

Box 4.5. Proposed Article on splitting and consolidation of cases

Splitting the case

"Article X. The district court may divide the case file where:

1. the proceedings are initiated following an appeal or a prosecutor protest against a decision under Article 58e by which the sanctioning authority has ruled on two or more violations committed in different judicial districts;
2. the proceedings are initiated following an appeal or a prosecutor protest against an act referred to in Article 58e by which the sanctioning authority has ruled on the liability of two or more persons who have acted without connection with each other;
3. the conditions for the stop of proceedings against one or more of the persons against whom an order under Article 58e has been issued are met, and the other conditions are not met."

Consolidation of cases

"Article X.

(1)The district court may combine two or more cases brought on appeal or prosecutor protest against decisions under Article e of the AVPA where :

1. has territorial jurisdiction to hear cases;
2. the judicial inquiry into either of them has not begun.

(2) The court shall exercise its powers under paragraph 1 where two or more of the acts referred to in Article 58e are issued against:

1. two or more persons for the same violation;
2. the same person for the same violation;
3. the same person for two or more violation committed in the same factual context."

Note: Provisions proposed by the OECD.

A separate but related issue pointed out in the Phase 4 report of the OECD Working Group on Bribery concerns the fact that, where sanctions against legal persons are imposed in the course of the criminal proceedings against natural persons, the AVPA provides for separate proceedings for natural and legal persons. While this is justified by judges participating in the review process with the fact that proceedings against legal persons tend to be faster and more flexible, and may continue independently in cases where the natural person is later acquitted, the report notes that evidence gathered in the criminal proceedings against natural persons may be used in the proceedings against legal persons and, more generally, that evidentiary activity on the two set of proceedings cannot be isolated. Based on this the report concludes that, where appropriate, Bulgaria consider combining proceedings against natural and legal persons in the same case following the practice of some other OECD Working Group members with non-criminal corporate liability. (OECD, 2021[1])

4.3. The AVPA could provide for the possibility to suspend proceedings in case of mental offender's disorder or if a request for international co operation is pending

Currently, the possibility to suspend the administrative penalty proceedings is regulated in Article 43, para. 6 of the AVPA, as follows:

> *When the offender, after a thorough inquiry, cannot be found it shall be noted in the act and the proceedings shall be terminated.*

This is the only hypothesis when the administrative penalty proceedings can be suspended, which is addressed later on in the report when discussing the servicing the summons, papers and notices (section 4.5) and the possibility of in absentia proceedings (section 4.11). Beyond this option, the legal framework could provide for the possibility to suspend proceedings in other cases such as when, after the offence has been committed, the offender has been affected by a short-term mental disorder, which precludes his sanity, and in cases where a response to a request for international co-operation is expected. In particular:

1. The offender's short-term mental disorder, which excludes his sanity after committing the violation, is not an obstacle to his administrative penalty liability. This circumstance only temporarily impedes his ability to participate in the proceedings and to exercise his right to defence. In case the person recovers, the sanctioning body would have the power to resume the proceedings and to ascertain the responsibility of the suspected offender. In case the person does not recover by the expiration of the limitation period, the sanctioning body should be obliged to terminate the proceedings.
2. If a response to a request for international co-operation related to summoning a person from another EU member state or obtaining evidence relevant to the subject of the file is expected, there is again reason to suspend the proceedings because no other procedural actions are required during this period, and because the suspension of the proceedings is necessary so that the preclusive term for issuing a penalty ruling provided for in Article 34 of the AVPA does not expire.

The power to suspend proceedings should belong to the sanctioning body and not, as before, to the authority which issued the act. On the one hand, the exercise of the power of suspension of the proceedings is a decision on the merits, which is solely a competence of the sanctioning authority. On the other hand, this creates a legal guarantee against possible illegal procedural actions on the part of the authority, which issued the act. A closely related gap concerns the lack of a procedure to resume the suspended administrative penalty proceedings, both when the grounds for suspension cease to exist and when there is a need to perform additional actions to collect evidence.

Legal amendments to address the gaps in this area could be establishes both under the current AVPA and in a future codification act. The provisions could be worded as proposed in Box 4.6.

Box 4.6. Proposed Articles 52a and 52b

"Article 52a.

(1) Within the period referred to in Article 52 (1), the penalty authority shall suspend the proceedings:

1. where, after the offence has been committed, the offender has experienced a short-term disorder of consciousness which excludes sanity or has any other serious illness which prevents the conduct of the proceedings;
2. the person against whom the act for establishment of the administrative violation has been drawn up is a foreign national with immunity from the administrative criminal jurisdiction of the Republic of Bulgaria;
3. while awaiting a reply to a request for international co-operation;
4. the person against whom the act for establishment of the administrative violation has been drawn up cannot be found at the address for summoning indicated by him, his residence in the country has not been established and his absence hinders the discovery of the objective truth.

(2) The existence of a ground for suspension of the administrative criminal proceedings in respect of the offender shall not preclude the continuation of the proceedings in respect of the sole trader or legal entity whose activity has been the subject of a failure to fulfil an obligation towards the State or a municipality.

(3) The sanctioning authority shall decide on a suspension of proceedings by means of a reasoned order, which shall contain:

1. the first name, forename, surname and function of the person who issued it;
2. the date of issue of the decree;
3. the date of the act on the basis of which the file was opened and the name, position and place of employment of the act issuer;
4. a description of the offence, the date and place where it was committed, the circumstances in which it was committed;
5. the legal provisions which have been infringed culpably;
6. the reasons justifying the suspension of proceedings and the legal basis thereof;
7. signature of the sanctioning authority.

(4) The order referred to in paragraph 2 shall not be subject to appeal or prosecutor protest.

(5) Where the proceedings are suspended pursuant to art. 1 par.1, the sanctioning authority shall check every six months whether the situation of the offender allows the proceedings to continue.

Article 52b. The sentencing authority shall reopen the suspended proceedings by reasoned order in the following cases:

1. the reason for suspension no longer applies;
2. there has been a need to carry out additional evidence-gathering measures.

(2) Where proceedings are resumed, Article 52a par.3 and par.4 shall apply accordingly.

(3) When reopening proceedings on the basis of art 1 par.1, upon the healing of the person, the sanctioning body shall exercise its powers under Article 52 within one month of the date of healing.

(4) Where, in the course of the suspended proceedings, the conditions for their termination are established, the sanctioning authority shall terminate the proceedings without reopening the proceedings."

Note: The texts are based on the provisions which have been discussed in the working group for drafting Law amendment of AVPA, adopted by the National Assembly at the end of 2020. This version proposes two new grounds for suspension of proceedings and supplementation under p. 2 and 4 of Art. 52a, para. 1, as well as a new para. 2 of the text.

4.4. The AVPA could provide for specific rules on translation and interpretation rights during proceedings

Other procedural areas where rules could be further clarified are the ones concerning the procedural representation of persons and for translation of documents of procedural significance.

In 2014, Directive 2010/64/EU of the European Parliament and of the Council of 20 October 2010 on the right to interpretation and translation in criminal proceedings was transposed into Bulgarian law by introducing, in Article 55 par. 4of the Code of Criminal Procedure governing the rights of the accused, a new paragraph 3 under which an accused person who does not speak Bulgarian has the right to interpretation and translation in criminal proceedings in a language which he understands. The defendant shall be provided with a written translation of the decree for bringing the accusations, of the court rulings for a constraint measure, of the act of indictment, of the judgment delivered, of the decision of the Court of appeal and of the decision of the cassation instance. A defendant shall be entitled to refuse written translation pursuant to this Code where he/she has a defence counsel and his/her procedural rights are not being violated.

However, there is no provision in AVPA on the right to translation of participants and before the court. Apart from this, the failure to ensure the right to translation at the out-of-court stage of the procedure may have an extremely negative impact on the rights of defence of the persons against whom an act for establishment of the administrative violation has been drawn up in the proceedings. To address these gaps it is necessary a set of provisions in the procedural law to be established.

In the first place, it is necessary to create a provision which explicitly states the language in which proceedings are conducted (Box 4.7).

Box 4.7. Proposed Article on language of proceedings

"Article X.

(1) The proceedings under this Act are conducted in Bulgarian.

(2) Persons who do not speak Bulgarian may use their native language or another language indicated by them. In these cases, an interpreter shall be assigned to the person.

(3) The sanctioning authority or the court appoints an interpreter in cases where it cannot itself verify the correctness of the translation of documents submitted in a foreign language.

(4) When a party to the proceedings is deaf, deafblind, or blind, an interpreter into sign Bulgarian language is appointed."

Note: This proposal is based on the draft Administrative Violations and Penalties Code of 2015.

Secondly, an explicit regulation of the rights of the person against whom the act for establishment of the administrative violation has been drawn up is necessary (Box 4.8).

Box 4.8. Proposed Article on the rights of the person against whom the act for establishment of the administrative violation has been drawn up

"Article X.

(1) The person against whom the act for establishment of the administrative violation has been drawn up shall be entitled to:

1. find out for what violation for the act was drawn up and on the basis of which evidence;
2. give or refuse to give explanations;
3. become familiar with the evidence collected and make the necessary extracts;
4. presents and requests the taking of evidence of its own motion;
5. be involved in the proceedings;
6. refuse to participate in separate actions of evidence collection;;
7. make requests, observations and objections;
8. appeals against acts which adversely affect his rights and legitimate interests;
9. be represented by a legal representative.

(2) The exercise of the right referred to in paragraph 1 item 9 shall not cause urgent actions to be delayed.

(3) The person against whom the act for establishment of the administrative violation has been drawn up, who does not have a command of Bulgarian, has the right to interpretation and translation in administrative penalty proceedings in a language which he understands.

(4) The person against whom the act for establishment of the administrative violation has been drawn up, shall be provided with a translation of the act, the final decision of the sanctioning authority and the decision of the district and administrative courts within 24 hours of their preparation. That person shall have the right to interpretation during interrogation and discussion of the terms of the agreement. The person against whom the act for establishment of the administrative violation has been drawn up may

refuse translation or interpretation when represented by a lawyer or legal adviser or other person with a legal background.

(5) The provisions of paragraphs 1 to 4 shall apply mutatis mutandis to the legal representative of the sole trader or the legal entity against whom the act for establishment of the administrative violation has been drawn up."

Note: Para.1, 2, and 5 build on art. 76, para. 1-3 of the draft Code of Administrative Penalties and Violations of 2015. Para. 3 and 4 are new proposals.

The need to regulate the issue of costs at the extra-judicial stage of the proceedings emerged during the interviews during the OECD fact-finding interview. In this context, it could be provide that the remuneration of experts, the interpreter and the interpreter in Bulgarian sign language should be determined by the act issuer, the sanctioning authority or the court, and that the costs are to be borne by the budget of the administration to which experts and interpreters are assigned.

It is also necessary for a provision similar to that of Article 142 of the Code of Criminal Procedure to be provided (Box 4.9).

Box 4.9. Proposed Article on witnesses' interpretation

"Article X.

(1) Where the witness does not have a command of the Bulgarian language, an interpreter is appointed.

(2) When the witness is deaf or silent, an interpreter in Bulgarian sign language is appointed.

(3) The rules of Article..... shall apply to the interpreter and interpreter in Bulgarian sign language.

(4) The hearing may also be carried out by a videoconference."

Note: This proposal is based on the draft Administrative Violations and Penalties Code of 2015.

4.5. Bulgaria could provide for more detailed and comprehensive rules for serving summonses, papers and notices in administrative penalty proceedings

Additional rules could be developed in the AVPA with regards to the serving of summonses and notices to the person against whom an act establishing an administrative violation is to be drawn up, or against whom an act has been drawn up and is to be filed and served. The only provision on these procedures is contained in the first subparagraph of Article 43, para. 4 of the AVPA. The same applies to the summoning of the persons against whom a penalty ruling has been issued according to Article 58, para. 1 of the AVPA. Furthermore, there are no special rules for the summoning of legal entities and sole entrepreneurs and of persons who have suffered damages as a result of the violation.

The respondents to the OECD questionnaire point out that the existing legal framework is insufficient to ensure the normal exercising of the powers of the controlling and sanctioning bodies to serve the relevant acts and the participation of legal entities in the out-of-court phase proceedings, for example in relation to the Traffic Law. A related issue has been raised by the OECD Working Group on Bribery, which expressed concern about the limited circumstances in which a legal person's representative is duly summonsed before court proceedings can commence and recommended that Bulgaria ensure that these limited circumstances do not prevent court proceedings against legal persons being commenced. (OECD, 2021[1]).

Participants to the workshop organised by the OECD to discuss preliminary recommendations proposed to simply the procedure for service of summonses and papers, especially in the cases when a low penalty is envisaged. Although this may be appealing it is important to ensure the same rules apply, since the right of defence and the right of the person to be informed of the penalty should not depend on the gravity of the violation and the amount of the sanction. However, legal changes on this topic is needed and the AVPA could provide for detailed rules for summoning and serving summonses, papers and notices, both to individuals and to sole entrepreneurs, legal entities and companies without legal personality.

Proposals in this direction were also made in the development of the latest amendments to the AVPA from the end of 2020, but their final adoption has not been achieved. Indeed, these rules need to be upgraded and their possible drafting could be as proposed in Box 4.10.

Box 4.10. Proposed Articles for serving summonses, papers and notices

"Article 43a.

(1) The summons for taking part in the proceedings and the service of documents and communications shall be implemented by:

1. the address for service or, if not found at these addresses, the permanent address and, for those registered in the BULSTAT register, at the address for correspondence entered in the register, for natural persons and, if they are abroad, service under the legal aid agreement with the State concerned or another mechanism of international law co-operation or, in the absence of a contract, through the Ministry of Foreign Affairs;
2. the address of the registered office for sole traders and legal entities, unless another address for correspondence is entered in the BULSTAT Register or another address is entered in the Commercial Register;
3. the address of the place of business, if there is no address referred to in subparagraph 2, for foreign persons doing business in the country through a permanent establishment or a fixed base;
4. the address declared to the offices responsible for the administrative control of foreigners — for a foreign national residing in the country, except in the cases referred to in subparagraphs 1 and 3;
5. the address of the first real estate acquired — for non-residents who have acquired real estate in the territory of the country and not covered by subparagraphs 1 to 4;
6. the place where a custodial sentence or detention order is to be served, for persons deprived of liberty and in custody;
7. to natural persons and legal entities registered in a foreign country for which the addresses referred to in points 2 3 to 5 are not available, service shall be effected in accordance with the legal aid agreement with the State concerned or any other mechanism of international law co-operation, or, where there is no contract, through the Ministry of Foreign Affairs.
8. By sending a message to a personal account registered in the secure electronic service information system as a module of the Single Portal for Access to Electronic Administrative Services within the meaning of the e-Government Act — where the person holds such an account.

(2) Persons requesting compensation and the other witnesses may also be summoned by telephone, telex or fax. The summons by telephone or fax shall be certified in writing by the official who did it and by telex with a written acknowledgement of receipt.

(3) Public enterprises, establishments or organisations harmed by the violation may be summoned via the e-mail address given in the case. An electronic message is deemed to have been served when the addressee sends an acknowledgement of receipt by means of a return electronic message, activation of a hyperlink or downloading it from the information system of the competent administration.

Article 43b.

(1) The summons is carried out by the act issuer or another person of the administration concerned. The summons shall include the act to which the person is summoned.

(2) A summons may be served by:

1. sending a letter with acknowledgement of receipt via a licensed postal operator, in which the action for summoning the person is written down.
2. via the municipality or town hall where the person has his address;
3. through the authorities of the Ministry of the Interior.

(3) A summons of a natural person may be served:

1. to the person, his or her representative or agent;
2. to an adult member of his household and to an adult having the same permanent address if they agree to accept it with the obligation to hand it over to the person;
3. at the place of work, either personally or through an employer or other employee, if he agrees to accept it under an obligation to hand it over;
4. if the person is deprived of his or her liberty or detained in custody, through the administration of the establishments concerned.

(4) A summons on a sole trader may be served to:

1. the sole trader;
2. his representative;
3. his employee, if he agrees to accept it with the obligation to hand it over to the person.

(5) A summons to a legal entity may be served to:

1. its manager or member of a management body;
2. his or her representative or agent;
3. his employee, if he agrees to accept it with the obligation to hand it over to the person.

(6) The official who served the summons shall return the receipt in a timely manner, which shall be placed on the file.

Article 43c.

(1) The person serving the summons shall certify by his signature the date and method of service, all acts of service, as well as his name and official capacity. He shall also record the full name, permanent address and capacity of the person to whom the summons was served, after requesting him to prove his identity by means of an identity document.

(2) The addressee of the summons certifies by his signature that he has received it.

(3) A summons sent by post with acknowledgement of receipt shall be deemed to have been served on the date on which the acknowledgement of receipt is signed by one of the persons referred to in Article 43b (4) to (6).

(4) Refusal to accept a summons shall be attested by the signature of the person who served it and at least one witness, mentioning the full name and permanent address or address of the summons and a note is taken on the receipt for this. Where service is effected through the municipality, town hall or licensed postal operator, the official concerned shall sign the refusal.

Article 43d.

(1) Service via attachment to the file shall be carried out:

1. in the case of natural persons, after at least two visits to the address to be summoned every 7 days, one of which during the weekend or, if he or she was not found, after one visit to his permanent address or address of work;
2. for sole traders and legal entities, after at least two visits to their registered office every seven days, in working days between 09.00 hours and 17.00 hours;
3. for foreign persons referred to in Article 43a (3) and (5), after at least two visits to the address every seven days, on working days between 09.00 hours and 17.00 hours, or, in the case of natural persons, after two visits to the address, one of which during the weekend.

(2) In case the person is not found on the addresses referred to in paragraph 1 during the second visit, the server shall place a notice at the entrance door informing him that the summons can be received within 14 days in the organisation to which the author belongs.

(3) The circumstances referred to in paragraphs 1 and 2 shall be attested by a record of each visit to the address, which shall include details of the time and place of the visit, the names, position and place of service of the person compiling it, the file on which it is drawn up, the date and time of the visit to the address, the activities carried out to visit the address and the signature of the person drawing it up. After completion of the procedure referred to in paragraphs 1 and 2, the act for establish the administrative violation shall be duly served on the date of the last visit to the address referred to in Article 43a.

(4) The requirements referred to in paragraph 1 shall not apply where there is clear evidence that:

1. the permanent address or address indicated for correspondence under Article 43a is non-existent;
2. the person has no permanent address or address for service in the country and his address abroad is not known.

(5) In the cases referred to in paragraph 4, the summons shall be placed in a designated place within the organisation to which the act issuer belongs. If the person fails to appear before the expiry of a period of 14 days from the date on which the summons was lodged, the summons shall be placed on the file and the document shall be deemed to have been duly served. The dates of affixing and downloading of the summons shall be recorded by the author on the summons itself.

Article 43e. The rules referred to in Articles 43a to 43d shall not apply where a special law provides otherwise."

Note: The texts are based on the provisions discussed in the working group for drafting Law amendment of AVPA, adopted by the National Assembly at the end of 2020, but these provision did not become part of the bill submitted to the National Assembly. The text propose a new version of Art. 43a, para. 1, 43b, para. 2 and Art. 43g, para. 2. Furthermore, items 7 and 8 are included in Art. 43a, para. 1, as well as para. 2 and 3 of Art. 43a.

The adoption of such a regulation will also lead to the repeal of the special rules for service of the penalty order referred to in Article 58 par.2 AVPA (SG. 109/2020 AVPA), the application of which, according to some of the respondents to the OECD questionnaire, gives rise to contradictory case-law. These proposed rule would contribute to address difficulties in summoning and serving documents to persons who do not have an address on national territory, which was also referred to as a problem in the data collection exercise as well as the concerns expressed by the OECD Working Group on Bribery on the limited circumstances for duly summonsing a legal person's representative. (OECD, 2021[1])

4.6. Bulgaria could introduce provisions on determining costs and remuneration in the out-of-court phase of the proceedings

The analysis of the legal framework also evidenced a possible gap in the law concerning the costs and remuneration in the out-of-court phase of the administrative penalty proceedings. Indeed, in this context there a two possible approaches.

The first one would be to consider that the costs incurred by the act issuer and the sanctioning authority during the pre-judicial stage of the proceedings in order to prove the violation and the identity of the offender remain at the expense of the establishment or organisation to which the sanctioning authority belongs, regardless of the act by which that stage of the proceedings ended. This is the current solution adopted by Bulgaria, which is similar to the one of Germany (Box 4.11).

Box 4.11. Settling costs in Germany

In Germany the following regulation applies in relation to costs according to Article 105 of the Act on Regulatory Offences:

"(1) In the proceedings of the administrative authority, section 464 subsections 1 and 2, sections 464a and 464c as far as the costs of sign language interpreters are concerned, sections 464d, 465, 466, 467a subsections 1 and 2, section 469 subsections 1 and 2, sections 470, 472b and 473 subsection 7 of the Code of Criminal Procedure shall apply mutatis mutandis, in the proceedings against juveniles and adolescents also section 74 of the Youth Court Act shall apply.

(2) The necessary expenses which the Treasury shall bear in accordance with subsection 1 in connection with section 465 subsection 2, section 467a subsections 1 and 2 as well as sections 470 and 472b of the Code of Criminal Procedure shall be imposed on the Federal Treasury if an administrative authority of the Federation conducts the proceedings, otherwise the Treasury of the Land shall bear the costs, unless otherwise provided by the law."

Source: OECD research.

The second one would be to assess whether the costs incurred in the pre-judicial phase of the proceedings may be charged to the offender in cases where the final law enforcement authority rules in favour of the question of his involvement in the violation for which the proceedings are initiated, where the proceedings end with a penal order, a warning under Article 28 AVPA or an agreement between the sanctioning authority and the offender. Should Bulgaria decide to take this approach, similar to the solution adopted by Austria, the possible legislative solution could as proposed in Box 4.13.

Box 4.12. Cost of the administrative penalty proceedings in Austria

"Article 64

(1) Each administrative penalty decision shall contain a clause stating that the person sentenced shall contribute a share of the cost of the penalty proceeding.

(2) This share amounts to 10% of the fine for the proceeding in first instance, however, to a minimum of EUR 10; in the case of detention sentences, one day of detention shall be deemed to be the equivalent of EUR 100. The share of cost paid

(3) Cash expenditures caused in the administrative penalty proceeding (Article 76) shall be reimbursed by the person sentenced, unless resulting from the fault of a different person; the amount to be reimbursed shall be quoted, whenever feasible, in the judgement (the decision), otherwise by separate administrative decision. This is not the case for any fees payable to interpreters and translators made available for the defendant.

(4) The collection of contributions to costs and cash outlays must be refrained from if there is reason to assume that it would be unsuccessful.

(5) Articles 14 and 54b (1), 1a and 1b are to be applied accordingly.

(6) If the offender's request to resume criminal proceedings is not granted, the preceding provisions shall apply mutatis mutandis to the obligation to bear the costs of the proceedings."

"Article 66

(1) In case a penalty proceeding is dropped or a sentence imposed is revoked because the proceeding is resumed, the costs of the proceeding shall be borne by the authority or refunded if already paid.

(2) In such cases the private prosecutor shall bear only such costs actually resulting from his intervention. (2) In such cases, the private prosecutor shall only be charged the costs actually caused by his intervention."

Source: Administrative Penalty Act of Austria.

Box 4.13. Proposed Articles on costs

"Article X.

(1) Costs in the procedure for finding an administrative offence and imposing an administrative penalty shall be met by the amounts provided for in the budget of the administration concerned, in which it is the authority ordered the action to be carried out.

(2) The remuneration of experts, the interpreter and the sign interpreter and the costs incurred by witnesses shall be determined by the act issuer or the sanctioning authority, via a decree.

(3) The costs of an interpreter and interpreter in Bulgaria sign language shall be charged to the budget of the administration to which they are assigned.

(4) The costs of witnesses and experts incurred in proving the offence shall be awarded to the person in respect of whom the order was made if the proceedings have resulted in a penalty order, caution or settlement. Where the act was issued in respect of several persons, the penalising authority or the court shall determine the portion to be paid by each of them (5) Where the proceedings are partially discontinued for one of the offences or one of the persons, the sanctioning authority shall order the person in respect of whom the proceedings are continued to pay only the costs incurred in proving the violation for which the proceedings culminate in a penal order, warning or settlement.

(6) When administrative penalty proceedings are terminated, the costs shall remain at the expense of the budget of the administration in which the sanctioning authority is located.

(7) For the costs awarded, a writ of execution is issued by the relevant court of first instance.

(8) The penalty order and the warning may also be appealed only in respect of the costs awarded."

Note: The text are based on Article 128 of the draft Code of Administrative Violations and Penalties of 2015. Provisions of para. 1, para. 2 (the costs for witnesses are also included), para. 4 et al. 6, as well as a new para. 8 are new proposals. The regulation of the costs awarded by the courts, proposed by the draft of Code, has not been recreated here, as the issue has been included in the AVPA with two consecutive amendments from 2019 and from 2020.

4.7. Bulgaria could ensure the coherency of procedural rules by applying rules of criminal procedure for both appeals and cassation proceedings for administrative penalty cases

A significant part of penalty orders are subject to appeal in front of judicial bodies (Figure 4.1). Penal orders are subject to challenge before the regional courts, which act as courts of first instance appeal in such proceedings. They review cases under the Criminal Procedure Code. At the same time, the decisions of the district courts are subject to cassation appeal before the administrative courts on the grounds, provided for in the Criminal Procedure Code (PPC) and following the procedure under Chapter Twelve of the Administrative Procedure Code (APC).

Figure 4.1. Appeals against penal orders in 2019

	Cassations appeals	First instance appeals	Total
Total number of penalty orders issued in 2019			590 536
Number of annuled penalty orders in 2019	6 839	9 703	16 542
Number of pending appeals in 2019	9 312	168 289	177 601
Number of amendments to penalty orders in 2019	2 077	11 433	13 510
Number of confirmed penalty orders in 2019	9 753	28 073	37 826

Source: 2019 Annual State of the Administration Report.

The reference to both the PPC and the APC in the current provision of Article 63, para. 1 of the AVPA creates a number of difficulties in the practice of administrative courts. One of the questions is whether in cassation proceedings the administrative court has the power to re-classify the violation described in the penal decree, bringing the facts established by the administrative sanctioning authority under another provision of law which has been infringed (point 2 of the proposal to institute interpretative case No 1/2020 of the Supreme Administrative Court's has not been decided yet). There is also the contradiction between the reference to Chapter Twelve of the Administrative Procedure Code and the reference to the provisions of the PPC in Article 84 of the AVPA in connection with unresolved issues related to the reviewing of cassation appeals by the administrative court.

In particular, Article 84 of the AVPA, following the last amendment in 2011, states that:

> *Inasmuch as this Act contains no special rules for subpoena and presentation of subpoena and announcements, making inventory lists and seizing objects, determining expenses of witnesses and remuneration of experts, calculation of periods, as well as for the proceedings in court for consideration of complaints against penal prescriptions, of cassation claims at the administrative court and proposals for resumption shall apply the provisions of the Penal Procedure Code.*

And in Article 63 (1), 2 (after amendment — Article 63c), it is stated that:

> *The decision of the Regional court shall be subject to cassation appeal before the Administrative court on the grounds, provided for in the Penal Procedure Code and under Chapter Twelve of the Administrative Procedure Code.*

The reference to two different procedural regulations applicable to the same procedure was not removed by the 2020 amending law, although in the course of the discussion preceding the submission of the draft law to the National Assembly, such proposals were made by interested parties. To address these inconsistencies, the AVPA could provide for the reference to the procedures laid down in the Code of Criminal Procedure only (Box 4.15). The procedure under the Code of Criminal Procedure should be preferred given the origins of the administrative penalty system in Bulgaria, whose structure and concepts derive from criminal law . Furthermore, this would be in line with the model adopted by Germany, which is also informed by criminal law and has been influencing Bulgaria's administrative penalties system since its inception Box 4.14.

Box 4.14. Use of criminal procedure rules throughout administrative penalty proceedings in Germany

In Germany, section 46 (1) of the Act on administrative penalties (OWiG) provides for the general rule of applicability mutatis mutandis of the general criminal law acts on the imposition of administrative penalties by administrative authorities. Section 67 of this act (OWiG) ensures the applicability mutatis mutandis of a few provisions of the German Code of Criminal Procedure (CCP). According to section 79, 80 and 80a OWiG the Administrative Penalty division (Bußgeldsenat) of the Higher Regional Courts (Oberlandesgericht) are in charge of judicial review of administrative decisions imposing administrative penalties, and they apply the German Code of Criminal Procedure.

Source: OWiG

Should Bulgaria decide to codify administrative penalty law, it should be recommended that the questions relating to the pleas in cassation and the procedure for dealing with the appeal on a point of law should be laid down in detail (see next para), avoiding a reference to procedural rules laid down in other legal acts which govern different procedural relationships in nature.

Box 4.15. Proposed Article 63(c)

"**Article 63c**. The decision of the district court shall be subject to appeal on a point of law before the administrative court, on the grounds and in accordance with the procedures laid down in the Code of Criminal Procedure."

Note: This is a new proposal from OECD.

4.8. Bulgaria could introduce regulation of the cassation review over the sanctioning acts of the administration

With the entry into force of the new amendments to the AVPA adopted in December 2020 the regulation of the judicial review of the sanctioning act of the administration was updated through explicit regulation of the powers of the district court, the procedural representation of the parties before the regional court and the regulation of abbreviated court proceedings

However, the AVPA has not yet regulated in detail the proceedings before the administrative (cassation) courts, so additional rules may be considered to clarify the grounds for cassation appeal and powers of the cassation court. A comprehensive regulation of cassation proceedings under the AVPA could be implemented by means of a comprehensive codification of the rules on administrative penalties. Concrete proposals were made with the 2015 draft Code of Administrative Violations and Penalties, which is the basis for the rules proposed in Box 4.16.

Box 4.16. Proposed Articles on cassation review

"**Chapter.........**

Cassation proceedings

Subject of the cassation proceedings

Art. 1. Subject to cassation proceedings entirely or in its separate parts shall be the first instance decision of the district court rendered by the order of art.63- 63b.

Right of cassation complaint or protest

Art. 2.

(1) The procedure before the cassation instance shall be instituted upon challenge of the prosecutor or upon appeal of the other parties.

(2) Right to appeal the decision shall have the parties or their legal representatives in the case, for which it is unfavourable.

(3) The prosecutor may submit cassation protest when his/hers procedural rights are violated and/or he/she finds that the rights and legal interests of one of the other parties are violated.

(4) A party that has not challenged the act under Art.58e AVPA before the district court could also file the cassation appeal or protest.

Cassation grounds

Art. 3.

(1) The decision of the district court be subject to cancellation or amendment under cassation procedure:

1. where the law is offended;
2. where a significant procedural breach has been admitted;
3. where the imposed penalty is obviously unjust.

(2) Offence of the law appears where it has been applied incorrectly or the law which shall be applied has not been applied.

(3) The breach of procedural rules shall be significant if:

1. has led to limitation of the procedural rights of the parties if has not been removed;
2. there is no reasons or a protocol of a district court;
3. the decision have been rendered by a non-lawful body;
4. the confidentiality of the deliberation has been broken during the rendering of the verdict or the decision.

(4) The procedural breach which cannot be removed does not establish ground for cancellation of the decision.

(5) The punishment is obviously unjust, if it is not relevant to the social danger of the violation and the perpetrator, to the extenuating and the aggravating the liability circumstances, as well as to the purposes of art.12 AVPA.

Term and order of submission of the cassation complaint and the prosecutor protest

Art. 4. The complaint and the protest shall be submitted within fifteen-day period from its announcement of the decision of the district court.

Contents of the complaint and the protest

Art. 5.

(1) the complaint or the protest shall be filed in written form and shall contain:

1. Indication of the district court through which the complaint or protest are filed;
2. Indication of the administrative court to which the complaint or protest are filed;
3. the name and the exact address of the appellant, respectively the name and the position of the prosecutor;
4. Indication of the appealed decision;
5. Precise and grounded indication of the concrete defects of the decision, which present cassation grounds;
6. What consist the claim of:

(2) The complaint or the protest shall be signed.

(3) To the complaint or the protest shall be attached:

1. document for paid state fee;
2. copies of the complaint or the protest according to the rest parties.

(4) An objection against a filed complaint and protest, as well as the amendment to them, could be made in writing until the case is heard in court.

Verification of jurisdiction

Art. 6.

(1) after initiating the case, the court shall check the jurisdiction.

(2) When the court finds that the case is not within its jurisdiction, it shall immediately send the case to the relevant administrative court.

(3) in cases under para.2 the term for filing the cassation appeal or protest shall be assessed as of the date of their submission to the court through which they are filed.

Verification of regularity

Art. 7.

(1) When the cassation complaint or protest do not meet the requirements under art. 5, para.1, letters 2-6 or para.2, they shall be left without movement, as the disputing party shall be given an opportunity to eliminate the irregularities within the 7- days period from the receipt of the notification thereof.

(2) The corrected contestation shall be considered regular from the day of its submission.

(3) If the irregularities are not eliminated within the term under para.1, the administrative court shall terminate the proceedings.

(4) The ruling of the administrative court under para.3 is final.

Admissibility verification

Art.8

(1) The administrative court shall terminate the proceedings when the cassation complaint or protest:

1. Has not been submitted in time;
2. Is filed by a person who has not right to appeal or protest;
3. Is not subject to consideration by cassation procedure.

(2) The ruling of the administrative court for termination of the proceedings shall be final.

Withdrawal and refusal from cassation contestation

Art. 9.

(1) The appellant may withdraw or refuse entirely or partially from the contestation till the finishing of the cassation proceedings.

(2) The legal representative may withdraw the complaint only with the consent of the person he represents.

(3) In the cases under art.1 the court shall declare the disputed act is entered into force and shall terminate the proceedings with a ruling, which shall be final.

(4) When the act is challenged by several persons and only one of them withdraws his complaint or protest, the proceeding in respect of the others shall not be terminated.

Procedure of consideration of the cassation complaint and the protest

Art. 10.

(1) the cassation complaint and the protest shall be considered in a Court session with summoning the parties.

(2) Non-appearance of one of the parties without good reasons shall not establish obstacle to try the case. The case shall be tried in the absence of the party, if the party has not been found at the indicated address.

(3) The chairman judge or reporting judge reports the content of the cassation complaint or protest.

(4) The parties shall be heard following an order as established by the Court.

Subject of the cassation check

Art. 11.

(1) The Administrative Court shall consider only the defects of the decision, pointed out in the complaint or the protest.

(2) The court shall also annul or amend the decision in respect of the undisputed parties, if the grounds for this are in their favour.

(3) The court shall check and ex officio for the significant violations of the procedural rules in the proceedings before the district court.

Evidence

Art. 12

(1) For the establishment of the cassation grounds shall be admitted written evidence.

(2) Shall not be admitted evidence for the establishment of circumstances, which are not related with the cassation grounds.

Prohibition for factual establishments

Art. 13. The Administrative Court shall assess the application of the material law on the ground of the facts, established by the first instance court in the appealed decision.

Powers of the administrative court

Art. 14.

(1) The administrative court shall pronounce within one month from the holding of the court session, in which the case has been announced for decision.

(2) The administrative court may:

1. annul the decision and confirm the act under art. 58e;
2. annul the decision and annul the act under art. 58d;
3. annul the decision and return the case to the district court;
4. amend the decision;
5. confirm the decision;
6. annul the decision of the district court and terminate the administrative penalty proceedings;
7. suspend the administrative penalty proceedings.

(3) The administrative court shall annuls the decision and confirms the act under art.58e, when there is a respective complaint or protest.

(4) The administrative court shall annuls the decision and remand the case back for new trial in the first instance, when:

1. a substantial violation of the procedural rules has been committed during its enactment;
2. a violation of a substantive law, which cannot be remedied by the administrative court, has been committed during its enactment;
3. ascertains that there is a ground under art. 63, para. 2, item 3, when the proceedings before the administrative court and before the district court have been instituted upon a respective protest of the prosecutor.

(5) The administrative court shall amend the decision, when a violation of a substantive law remediable by the administrative court has been admitted and there is a ground under art. 63, para. 2, items 1, 2 or 4.

(6) The administrative court shall confirm the decision when there are no grounds for its annulment or amendment.

(7) The administrative court shall revoke the decision and shall terminate the administrative penalty proceedings when it establishes that after issuing the disputed judicial act a circumstance under Art. 34, b. "A" - "c".

(8) The decision of the administrative court shall be final.

(9) The administrative court shall suspend the dispute proceedings when:

1. one of the parties in the proceedings has fallen into a short-term or long-term disorder of consciousness, which excludes sanity or has another serious illness, which prevents the participation in the proceedings;

2. while awaiting a response to a request for international co-operation.
3. After the grounds for suspension have ceased to exist, the court shall resume the administrative penalty proceedings with a ruling.

Mandatory instructions

Art. 15

(1) Upon the review of the case, the instructions of the cassation instance shall be mandatory with regard to:

1. the application of the law, save in the cases where other states of facts have been established;
2. removal of the admitted significant breaches of procedural rules.

(2) Elimination of the admitted significant violations of procedural rules.

(3) The instructions of the administrative court shall be obligatory.

Special provision

Art. 16. For matters not covered by this Chapter, the rules of…shall be applied."

Note: These proposals are based on the draft Administrative Violation Code of 2015.

These rules would maintain the competence of administrative courts over cassation proceedings as this is part of a broader judicial policy of Bulgaria. However, a reflection and discussion could start among representatives of the executive and judicial branches to evaluate advantages and disadvantages of maintaining the current division of competence or transfer the cassation review back to the district courts. The comparative experience seems to go into the direction of having either administrative or criminal judges reviewing administrative penalties at the appeals and cassation levels (Box 4.17).

Box 4.17. Judicial review of administrative penalties in Austria, Czech Republic and France

Austria

The decisions to impose a sanction are subject to full judicial review by the administrative jurisdiction. First, the Federal Finance Court, the Federal Administrative Court or one of the nine regional administrative courts are responsible for the appeals/complaints. As a rule, these courts have to hold a public, oral hearing. These courts have full cognitive power and decide in administrative penalty matters always in the matter itself. These decisions are subject to a legal control by the Supreme Administrative Court or the Constitutional Court.

Czech Republic

A decision imposing a sanction for an administrative offense may be challenged by a complaint under Section 65 of Act No. 150/2002 Coll., which is decided by a regional court in administrative judiciary. The decision of the regional court may be challenged by a cassation complaint to the Supreme Administrative Court. The court examines the legal and factual circumstances of the case (it may, for example, repeat or add evidence produced by the administrative body - Section 77 (2) of Act No. 150/2002 Coll.).

France

There are several means of appeal that allow administrative sanctions to be reviewed by the administrative judge. The person to whom the administration has imposed a sanction may challenge it before the administrative judge, by means of the various appeal procedures that are the recourse for excess of power and the recourse for full litigation. The recourse available depends on the type of sanction contested, it being noted that the scope of the full recourse is extensive.

Source: (European Committee on Crime Problems, 2020[2]).

4.9. Bulgaria could introduce additional possible grounds to resume proceedings before the entry into force of the penal order

One of the points raised by public entities during the workshop was how to proceed in case, after the issuance of the final act of the sanctioning authority and before the initiation of a judicial review of this act, a legal basis for termination occurs, i.e. death of the offender, expiration of the statute of limitations, deletion of the sole proprietorship/legal entity.

Detailed regulation of the powers of the district court in the proceedings for judicial control over the acts of the sanctioning body partly addressed this issue. According to new amendment law the court has the power to revoke the act under Art. 58e and to terminate the administrative penalty proceedings (Art. 63, para. 6, item 2, item 3 AVPA) in case the death of the person or termination of legal entity occurs after issuance of penal order. However, there is still legislative gap in cases when the person has died or the legal entity has been terminated after issuance - but before the entry into force - of a penal order. In this case the penal order will enter into force.

Considering this gap a new ground for resuming proceedings could be included. This should be a possibility, but not obligation for the prosecutor: if the prosecutor considers that there are no grounds for resumption, the act will enter into force and will give rise to its legal consequences in the legal sphere of the person's heirs. It is not necessary in any of the cases to reopen the proceedings, because if the violation is established in an unequivocal manner and no substantial violation of the procedural rules is committed, it is logical for the legal entity to be sanctioned, even if the fine is collected from the property, left after his death. However, there should also be the possibility of resuming the proceedings where there are the reasonable grounds that the penalty order could be revoked and there is no other option for that because of the death of sanctioned person or termination of the legal entity within the period between the issuance of penal order and enter into force.

4.10. Bulgaria could consider discontinuing the possibility to settle civil claims in administrative penalty proceedings

According to the provisions of Article 45, para. 1 of the AVPA, in its current wording, until the penalty ruling is issued, the victim can submit a request to the sanctioning body for compensation for damages to the amount of up to two BGN (in comparison, up to 01.05.2021 the minimal salary set for the country is in the amount of BGN 650), unless the relevant law or decree provides for the possibility of claiming a larger compensation for damages before the same body.

The possibility for a person who has suffered harm as a result of the violation to bring a civil action for damages in the course of administrative criminal proceedings derives from the general principle of law that everyone is obliged to repair the damage wrongfully caused by them to someone else. Where the offence is also a tort, the injured party has two possibilities: to bring a civil action for recovery of the damage caused to them before the civil court, in accordance with the Code of Civil Procedure, or to submit a claim for compensation to the sanctioning authority.

Despite the relatively detailed arrangements for civil claim in administrative criminal proceedings, the analysis of administrative penalty cases shows that this provision does not find real practical application for two reasons: first, due to the principle that administrative violations affect the established order of government, therefore they may not cause substantial damage to individual citizens or economic operators, and secondly, due to the outdated amount of compensation for damages that can be claimed under this order.

This conclusion is also based on the answers to during the OECD fact-finding mission whereas interviewees have not been able to rule on a civil claim brought jointly with administrative criminal proceedings, and they agree that dealing with a civil claim, especially for compensation for material damage, would constitute a significant difficulty for them, as it would require an assessment of whether the violation concerned has caused damage, of what type and to what extent. Bulgaria could thus consider discontinuing the possibility of examining a civil claim in administrative criminal proceedings. A number of recommendations have also been made in the course of the discussion for the draft of AVPA adopted at the end of 2020. This can be achieved by repealing Articles 45 and 55 of the AVPA and amending the other provisions of the Act governing the procedural rights of the victim.

4.11. Bulgaria could introduce the possibility of in absentia proceedings in specific cases to avoid delays and impunity

Most of the respondents to the OECD questionnaire have pointed out that a serious problem for engaging the responsibility of legal entities is establishing their current location, their summoning to participate in the proceedings, respectively presenting and serving the drafted act. It is pointed out that in many cases the violators do not want to receive summonses and messages, they do not appear when summoned, and their current address cannot be established. This significantly delays the administrative penalty proceedings and creates impunity.

According to current art. 43, para. 6 of the AVPA, when the violator cannot be found after a thorough search, this shall be noted in the act and the proceedings shall be suspended. The administrative penalty authorities have faced the same problem. In art. 58, para. 2, however, when the offender or the person requesting compensation is not found at the address indicated by them, and their new address is unknown, the sanctioning body shall mark this in the penalty ruling and it shall be considered served from the day this has been marked.

Provisions for the default service of administrative infringement notices issued and penalty orders issued are also laid down in the special administrative legislation such as:

- Article 233 par.4 of the Consumer Protection Act, which provides that notices establishing administrative violations and penal orders within the meaning of the Administrative Violations and Penalties Act, as well as individual administrative acts within the meaning of the Administrative Procedure Code, may be served to any natural person who is in the business premises and who has a civil or employment relationship with the person against whom they are issued.
- Article 232 of the Customs Act, which lays down two exceptions to the rules on the lodging and service of the document and the penal order. Where the offender is unknown, the act is to be signed by the act issuer and one witness and not to be served. In this case, a penal order shall be issued, which shall take effect from the time it is issued. Where the offender is known but not found at the address indicated when the administrative offence was served, or has left the country, or has indicated an address abroad only, the law again provides that the penal order shall not be served and shall be deemed to have entered into force two months after it was issued.

In this context, Bulgaria could consider introducing limited cases in which the proceedings may continue, even if the offender is not found to be presented and served the act. A similar possibility is regulated for the persons who have committed a crime in art. 269 of the Criminal Procedure Code and in other EU countries (Box 4.18).

Box 4.18. Proceedings in absentia in Austria and Germany

Austria

The Austrian regulation on Administrative Penalties (VwSG) limits the requirement to hear the accused to the obligation to give him the opportunity to react in writing before the given time limit (see Article 42, second paragraph). The relevant provisions on the obligation to hear the accused are the following:

"Article 40

(1) f the authority does not already dispense with prosecution on basis of the data in the report received or of the results of the investigation carried out (§ 45), it shall give the defendant an opportunity to present his case.

(2) For this purpose, the authority may summon the accused to be questioned or request him to either appear at a certain point in time for questioning or to justify himself in writing by this point in time. In doing so, the accused is to be informed of his right to call in a defence counsel of his choice for questioning.

(3) If the accused is not in the municipality in which the authority has its seat, it can arrange for the accused to be questioned by the municipality of his place of residence.

Article 41

(1) The summons (§ 19 AVG) must contain:

1. the clear description of the offense against which the accused is charged and the administrative regulation in question;
2. the request to present the facts useful for the defence and to bring the evidence useful for the defence or to inform the authority in good time that they can still be brought for questioning.

(2) The summons can also contain the threat that the criminal proceedings can be carried out without a hearing if the accused does not comply with the summons without justification. This legal consequence can only occur if it is threatened in the summons and if the summons has been served on the accused in his own hands.

Article 42

(1) The request pursuant to Section 40 (2) must contain:

1. the clear description of the offense against which the accused is charged and the administrative regulation in question;
2. the request to justify oneself in writing within the set deadline or orally at the time specified for questioning and to disclose the facts and evidence serving the defence to the authority, otherwise the authority will conduct the criminal proceedings without his hearing.

(2) This request must be sent to your own hands."

Germany

According to Article 74 of Germany´s Act on Regulatory Offences:

"(1) The main hearing shall be conducted in the absence of the person concerned if he has not appeared and was relieved of the obligation of personal appearance. Previous examinations of the person concerned and his statements put on record and other statements shall be introduced at the main hearing by communication of their essential content or by reading them out. It shall suffice to give defence counsel the indications required in accordance with section 265 subsections 1 and 2 of the Code of Criminal Procedure.

(2) If the person concerned fails to appear without sufficient excuse although he was not relieved of the obligation to appear, the court shall reject the objection in a judgment without a hearing on the merits.

(3) In the summons the person concerned shall be informed of subsections 1 and 2 and section 73 and section 77b subsection 1 first and third sentences.

(4) If the main hearing has been held without the person concerned in accordance with subsection 1 or 2 he may, in respect of the judgment, request within one week of service restoration of the status quo ante on the same conditions as apply in respect of failure to observe a time limit. He shall be informed thereof upon service of the judgment."

Source: OECD Research

4.12. Bulgaria could introduce provisions to ensure compliance with administrative penalties imposed by a foreign countries and to establish international co-operation

The AVPA does not contain provisions regulating the execution of penalties imposed abroad or the execution abroad of penalties imposed by Bulgarian administrative bodies. Furthermore, as some of the respondents to OECD questionnaire have pointed out, the issue of international legal co-operation in administrative penal cases is becoming more and more relevant. The number of cases of violations of cross-border nature or committed by foreign citizens or Bulgarian citizens with permanent residence in another country is increasing. This is particularly relevant for legal entities without a registered office and address in Bulgaria, as well as for violations that have affected a Bulgarian citizen or violated the interests of the Bulgarian state or a Bulgarian municipality.

The legal framework could thus explicitly regulate these cases, including when another EU member state or a third country has imposed an administrative penalty for a violation that is subject to sanction or has already been sanctioned by the Bulgarian law enforcement authorities. In this sense, the draft Code of Administrative Violations and Penalties of 2015 proposed a regulation of international legal co-operation in administrative penalty proceedings which Bulgaria could consider to regulate this are (Box 4.19). However, before recommending such provisions to be adopted in the AVPA or in the relevant codification act, a deeper exploration of the opportunities for collaboration between the different administrations and the relevant competent bodies from other countries is necessary, both at the pre-judicial stage of the procedure and at the enforcement stage.

Box 4.19. Proposed regulation of international legal co-operation in administrative penalty proceedings

"Basis and content

Article 251.

(1) International legal assistance in administrative penalty proceedings shall be subject to an international agreement to which the Republic of Bulgaria is a party or to the principle of reciprocity.

(2) International legal aid includes:

1. service of documents;
2. collection of evidence;
3. provision of information;
4. other forms of legal aid provided for in an international treaty to which the Republic of Bulgaria is a party or imposed on a reciprocal basis.

An inquiry to the requested State

Article 252.

(1) The request for international legal aid shall contain:

1. the name of the authority making the request;
2. details of the authority competent to execute the inquiry of the requested State;
3. a description of the subject matter and the reason for the request;
4. the name and nationality of the person concerned by the request;
5. the name and address of the person on whom the documents are to be served;
6. where appropriate, a summary of the circumstances of the infringement and the legal provisions infringed.

(2) The request for international legal assistance shall be sent through the Ministry of Justice, unless an international treaty to which the Republic of Bulgaria is a party provides otherwise.

Execution of an inquiry from the requesting State

Article 253.

(1) The request for international legal assistance shall be sent to the Ministry of Justice, unless an international treaty to which the Republic of Bulgaria is a party provides otherwise.

(2) The request for international legal assistance shall be executed in accordance with the procedure laid down in Bulgarian law or in accordance with an international treaty to which the Republic of Bulgaria is a party.

(3) The request may also be executed in accordance with the procedure laid down by the law of the requesting State if this is requested and is not contrary to Bulgarian law.

(4) The requesting State shall be informed of the time and place of execution of the inquiry if so requested.

Refusal of international legal assistance

Article 254.

International legal assistance may be refused where the execution of the request could jeopardise sovereignty, national security, public order or other important interests protected by the law.

Costs of enforcement

Article 255. The costs of the execution of the request shall be apportioned between the parties in accordance with international treaties to which the Republic of Bulgaria is party or in accordance with the principle of reciprocity.

Article 256 (1) The provisions of Articles 251 to 255 shall not apply where a special law provides otherwise.

(2) The provisions of the Code of Criminal Procedure shall apply to matters not covered by Articles 251 to 255."

Source: This proposal is based on the draft Administrative Violations and Penalties Code of 2015.

In developing such regulation, Bulgaria could also consider the broader European context of mutual assistance in administrative penalty cases, as well as examples of regulations from single countries (Box 4.20).

Box 4.20. International co-operation in Europe and specific regulations in Germany and Austria

At the European level, a system of international co-operation in administrative penalty cases is lacking. Only recently the European legislator seems to pay attention to the lacking system of mutual assistance at the imposition and recovery of administrative pecuniary sanctions and the service of documents. According to EU law national authorities are increasingly obliged to loyally offer mutual assistance at the impositions of administrative pecuniary sanctions in an increasing amount of policy fields.

As far as administrative penalties are involved two systems of mutual assistance exits: a system of mutual assistance in criminal matters and a system of mutual assistance in administrative matters. Considering administrative penalties imposed by administrative authorities, the criminal law system applies when judicial review is offered by criminal courts and the administrative law system applies when judicial review is offered by administrative courts. Both systems exist in Europe and sometimes mutual assistance is required between two different national systems. European law requires national authorities to effectively co-operate with both systems, even if the national system of the requesting state is different from the national system of the requested state.

Administrative penalties imposed according to the German Act on administrative penalties fall within the ambit of systems of mutual assistance in criminal matters, such as the Framework Decision 2005/214 on the application of the principle of mutual recognition to financial penalties. Indeed, it is possible to provide legal assistance in "criminal matters" regardless of whether the offence in question is regulated by criminal or administrative procedure. The Act on International Legal Assistance in Criminal Matters [Gesetz über die internationale Rechtshilfe in Strafsachen – IRG] explicitly includes administrative offences provided that a court of criminal jurisdiction can determine the sentence (section 1 (2) IRG, comparable to Article 1 (3) of the Second Additional Protocol to the European Convention on Mutual Assistance in Criminal Matters (ETS 082)). This means that, as a rule, all instruments of legal assistance can be called upon for international co-operation in matters of criminal law.

As this framework decision is part of the system of mutual assistance in criminal cases most if not all Member States have implemented this European Regulation in their national criminal law systems. In Germany this is the Act on international mutual assistance in criminal matters (Gesetz über die internationale Rechtshilfe in Strafsachen (IRG)). In the Czech Republic this is § 460o ff of the Code of criminal procedure. In the Netherlands the framework decision was implemented with the "Wet wederzijdse erkenning en tenuitvoerlegging geldelijke sancties en beslissingen tot confiscatie". This is a special act which should be considered part of the national system of mutual assistance in criminal matters. Interestingly enough the case law following the Baláž-case encouraged the Dutch legislator to add administrative financial penalties which are part of the administrative law to the list of sanctions Dutch authorities are given the power to request assistance to authorities of other EU Member States. These only involve Dutch provisions falling with the ambit of 'conduct which infringes road traffic regulations, including breaches of regulations pertaining to driving hours and rest periods and regulations on hazardous goods' (see article 5, first paragraph, Framework Decision 2005/214).

In Austria the „Bundesgesetz über die justizielle Zusammenarbeit in Strafsachen mit den Mitgliedstaaten der Europäischen Union" (EU-JZG) applies to mutual assistance in criminal matters, whereas the EU-Verwaltungsstrafvollstreckungsgesetz applies to mutual assistance in matters of administrative penalties. This means that in Austria international mutual assistance regarding criminal financial penalties will be given on the basis of the EU-JZG whereas international mutual assistance regarding administrative financial penalties will be given on the basis of the EU-Verwaltungsstrafvollstreckungsgesetz. Mutual assistance requested by another member state on the basis of a legal instrument of mutual assistance in criminal matters, even if they involve administrative financial penalties imposed by administrative authorities, will follow the rules of the EU-JZG if judicial review is given by the criminal courts. If this act does not apply, the EU-Verwaltungsstrafvollstreckungsgesetz applies to the enforcement of administrative penalties requested by administrative authorities of other EU Member States. Requests of assistance of Austrian authorities to authorities of other EU Member States in matters concerning administrative penalties are regulated by this EU-Verwaltungsstrafvollstreckungsgesetz.

Source: OECD Research; (European Committee on Crime Problems, 2020[2]).

4.13. Bulgaria could introduce more detailed rules on the procedure to collect sanctions and to develop a mechanism to collect costs and pecuniary sanctions in administrative penalty cases from foreigners without permanent or known address in Bulgaria

According to Art. 79, para. 1 of AVPA, the penal decrees and decisions of the court, by which fines have been imposed or monetary compensations have been awarded in favour of the state, shall be fulfilled by the order of collecting the state takings. This is also the procedure established for the collection of the fine imposed as a penalty under the Criminal Code. In particular, Article 416, para. 4 of the Criminal Procedure Code, establishes that when the sentence includes a pecuniary sanction or compensations, or if court costs and fees are awarded in favour of the state, the court issues a writ of execution and sends it to the respective enforcement body.

The body authorised to collect state takings is the National Revenue Agency, which, however, does not have the competence to carry out actions for compulsory collection of debts arising from fines or pecuniary sanctions imposed on foreigners who have no permanent or known address in the Republic of Bulgaria and legal entities who have their registered office and address abroad. Indeed, neither the Criminal Procedure Code nor the Law on Administrative Offences provides for rules for the execution of sentences and rulings when the person against whom they are issued is a foreigner without permanent or known address in the Republic of Bulgaria. The only provision to that sense is that laid down in Article 79a of the AVPA, according to which, "when with the penal decree a pecuniary sanction was imposed to an offender without permanent address in the Republic of Bulgaria, the offender shall transfer the sum to an account noted in the penal decree." As a consequence, Bulgaria could develop a mechanism for collecting costs and pecuniary sanctions in administrative penalty cases from foreigners without permanent or known address in the territory of the Republic of Bulgaria.

Additionally, if the fine is not paid within a specified period, the debt is sent to the National Revenue Agency (´NRA´) for enforcement. However, if after that, the fine is paid to the authorities issuing the fine, they do not have the obligation to notify the NRA. As highlighted during the fact-finding interviews, this gaps creates a problem – in practice - because the debt is paid but the NRA continues the process to collect it. This situation does not only lead into a duplication of efforts, but it also creates uncertainty in citizens and businesses, which eventually undermines their trust in the enforcement system as a whole efficiency. To address this challenge, Bulgaria could introduce the compulsory notification, for the authority issuing the penal decree to notify the NRA if payment of the fine has been received, so that the NRA can terminate the proceedings to collect the fine. It is necessary also to be provided for an obligation of NRA to notify the authority issuing the penal decree in case the sanction has been collected.

In order to address these challenges, which were also pointed out in OECD questionnaires and interviews, the AVPA could be amended as proposed in Box 4.21.

Box 4.21. Proposed Article 79 and Article 79(a) of the AVPA

"Article 79

Art. 79. (1) Penal orders and court decisions by which fines or pecuniary sanctions have been imposed, or pecuniary compensation has been awarded in favour of the State, shall be executed in accordance with the procedure for the collection of State claims.

(2) In the event that enforcement proceedings are instituted for the collection of fines or pecuniary sanctions imposed:

1. the penalizing authority shall immediately notify the revenue authority, respectively the public executor, of the amounts collected;
2. the revenue authority or the public enforcement officer, as the case may be, shall immediately notify the penalising authority of the amounts collected.

(3) Penalty decrees and court decisions awarding monetary compensation in favour of state enterprises, cooperatives or other public organisations or citizens shall be enforced in accordance with the procedure provided for in the Code of Civil Procedure.

Article 79a.

(1) Where a penal order or a court decision imposes a pecuniary sanction on an offender without a fixed or current address in the Republic of Bulgaria, or on an offender with the address or residence in another country, the sanctioning authority or court may:

1. order the provisional execution of the punishment imposed;
2. collect the administrative pecuniary sanction imposed in accordance with the rules on international co-operation — except in the cases referred to in point 1.

(2) Enforcement of the punishment imposed shall be permitted where all the following conditions are met:

1. the offender has participated in the procedure for establishing an administrative offence and imposing an administrative penalty and the penal order or court decision issued has been duly served on him;
2. the offender agrees to pay the administrative pecuniary sanction imposed on him at the time of service of the penalty order or the court's decision.

(3) In case of provisional enforcement of the administrative penalty imposed, the offender is liable to pay 80% of the amount of that penalty. The penal order or the decision of the court in respect of which provisional enforcement has been granted shall be subject to appeal in accordance with Article 59. The pecuniary sanction imposed by a penal order or decision of the court which has been granted provisional enforcement, which has been appealed and confirmed by the court, is due in full.

(4) The administrative pecuniary sanction imposed, other than in the cases referred to in paragraph 1 (1), shall be collected:

1. under the procedure laid down in the Act on the recognition, execution and transmission of confiscation or confiscation orders and orders imposing financial penalties;
2. in accordance with bilateral or multilateral agreements on the enforcement of administrative pecuniary sanctions, except in the cases referred to in subparagraph 1;
3. by other appropriate means — except in the cases referred to in points 1 and 2

(5) The provisions of paragraphs 1 to 4 shall also apply mutatis mutandis to financial penalties imposed."

Note: These proposals are based on the new amendment of art.79b of AVPA but with some additions and improvements based on proposals suggested during the fact-finding interviews with Bulgarian entities.

4.14. The AVPA could introduce more detailed provisions on preclusive time periods and statutory limitations and ensure a differentiated regime in line with their functions

The regime on preclusive time periods and statutory limitations is regulated by Art. 34 AVPA.

According to some respondents to the OECD questionnaire, the one-year period in Article 34, para. 1 (c) AVPA for initiating administrative criminal proceedings in some cases is too short, also taking into account that there is no provision in the AVPA analogous to Article 81 para of the Criminal Code laying down an absolute limitation period after which administrative liability is extinguished, depending on the severity of legislative sanction provided by law but not on the penalty imposed.

In order to address these weakness Bulgaria could firstly establish a clear definition of preclusive time periods and statutory limitation periods. Preclusive time periods should have a disciplinary effect on the administration in order not to cause undue delays in proceedings and expiry of statutory limitation periods. The increase in the length of the period aims to guarantee that the evidence shall be lawfully gathered and, if the violation is established at the time it is committed or it is proved in a short time, it would not preclude to establish the liability in a shorter period of time.

Secondly, in order to address a challenge pointed out in Interpretative Decree No 1 of 27.02.2015 of the Supreme Court of Cassation and the Supreme Administrative Court, there should be a differentiation between ordinary limits (which may suspend and interrupted) and absolute limits (which are not affected by suspension and interruption).

Thirdly, the limitation period should be explicitly regulated for the attempt to commit an administrative violation that is punishable in the cases referred to in Article 9 para. 1 AVPA, as well as in the case of an offence of negligence (for example, failure to submit a declaration, failure to co-operate and the like). Limitation periods also need to apply to the liability of sole traders and legal entities. Until now, the principle of limitation applied to the category of legal entities analogically.

Based on these recommendations the wording of the relevant provisions could be amended as proposed in Box 4.22.

Box 4.22. Proposed Article 34 and 34a

"Article 34.

(1) Administrative penalty proceedings shall not be opened, and the opened ones shall be terminated if an act for establishment of the administrative violation has not been drawn up for the duration of:

1. six months from finding the offender, for violations of a legislative act governing the budgetary, financial and accounting activities referred to in Article 32 par.1, item 1 of the Public Financial Inspection Act, as well as for violations of a statutory instrument regulating the gambling activity and the measures against money laundering and terrorist financing, as well as for violations of the Energy Sector Act, the Energy from Renewable Sources Act and their implementing regulations, of Regulation (EU) No 1227/2011 of the European Parliament and of the Council of 25 October 2011 on wholesale energy market integrity and transparency as well as the ones for violation of the Independent Financial Audit Act.
2. four months from finding the offender for customs, taxation, ecological and foreign currency violations, as well as according to the Election Code, the Political Parties Act, the Public Offering of Securities Act, Markets in Financial Instruments Act, Special Investment Companies and Securitization Companies Act, the Act on Application the Measures Against Market Abuse with

Financial Instruments, Regulation (EU) no. 596/2014 of the European Parliament and of the Council of 16 April 2014 on market abuse (Regulation on Market Abuse) and repealing Directive 2003/6/EC of the European Parliament and of the Council and Directives 2003/124/EC, 2003/125/EC and 2004/72/EC of the Commission (OJ, L 173/1 of June 12, 2014), the Act on the Operation of the Collective Investment Schemes and of Other Undertakings for Collective Investment, Part Two, Part Two "A" and Part Three of the Code of Social Insurance, the Insurance Code and the statutory instrument for its implementation and under the Register BULSTAT Act

3. three months from the finding the offender, in other cases.

(2) Administrative penalty proceedings shall be terminated if no penal decree has been issued within six months from the date when the act of the establishment of the administrative violation was drawn up.

(3) Where proceedings are initiated pursuant to Article 36 para. 2, they shall be terminated if no penal decree has been issued within six months of receiving the materials by the court or prosecutor.

(4) The time limit referred to in paragraphs 2 and 3 shall not run while the proceedings are suspended.

Article 34a.

(1) Administrative penalty proceedings shall not be opened, and the opened ones shall be terminated when:

1. the offender has died;
2. the offender has lapsed into a permanent mental disorder;
3. the statutory limitation period has expired.

(2) Administrative criminal liability shall be time-barred if no administrative penalty has been imposed or a warning addressed to the offender in accordance with Article 28 by a final decision until the expiration of:

1. three years from the commission of the violation — for a violation under Article 34 para 1, item 1 and for violations punishable by a penalty of unpaid work for the benefit of the society
2. two years after the offence was committed, in the case of a violation under Article 34 para 1, item 2;
3. one year after the violation was committed, in other cases.

(3) For an attempt, the limitation period referred to in paragraph (2) shall begin on the day when the last act was carried out.

(4) The limitation period shall be suspended when:

1. the initiation or continuation of administrative criminal proceedings depends on the resolution of a preliminary matter by a final judicial decision. Once the question has been resolved by a final judicial decision, the limitation period continues to run.
2. the sanctioning authority has terminated the administrative criminal proceedings and has sent the materials to the prosecutor in accordance with the procedure laid down in Article 33 (2). In the event that the public prosecutor refuses to initiate pre-trial proceedings on the basis of the documents in the file or terminates the pre-trial proceedings initiated, the limitation period shall continue to run from the date on which the prosecution authority was seized by the public prosecutor.

(5) The statutory limitation period shall be interrupted in the case of:

1. drawing up an act for establishment of the administrative violation;
2. the lodging claiming and servicing of the act for establishment of the administrative violation;
3. adjudication by decision of the sanctioning authority in the administrative penalty file;
4. handling to the offender of the penalty decree or proposal referred to in Article 28;
5. the making of a decision or order by the court in proceedings under this legislative act.
6. summons of the offender to participate in the proceedings.

(6) After completion of the action, whereby statutory limitation was interrupted, a new limitation term shall start.

(7) Notwithstanding the suspension or interruption of the limitation period, administrative liability shall expire if four years and six months have elapsed since the violation was committed.

(8) The provisions of paragraphs 2 to 7 shall also apply mutatis mutandis to the liability of sole traders and legal entities.

(9) The provisions of Articles 1 to 8 shall apply unless a special law provides otherwise."

Note: A text with a similar wording has been discussed by the working group for the preparation of the Law of amendment and supplementation of AVPA adopted by the National Assembly at the end of 2020, promulgated, SG, issue 109 of 2020, but did not become part of the final bill submitted to the National Assembly. Paragraphs 3 and 4 are in the wording proposed by the OECD.

The establishment of provisions in the general law which exclude its application in special situations is necessary to ensure that special legislation takes into consideration sector specificities. Such longer time periods are laid down, for example, in Article 153 of the Credit Institutions Act, according to which acts for the establishment of the administrative violation shall be drawn up by officials authorised by the deputy manager of the Banking Supervision Administration within one year of the day on which the offender is found, but no later than 5 years after the violation was committed.

The Act amending and supplementing the Payment Services and Payment Systems Act, promulgated in SG No 13/2020, provides in Article 188 (1) that the acts for the establishment of the administrative violation under Articles 187-185 shall be drawn up by persons authorised by the deputy manager of the Bulgarian National Bank managing the „Bank Supervision" within 6 months of the day on which the offender was found, but no later than 5 years after the offence was committed, and penal orders shall be issued by the deputy manager or by a person authorised by him.

Should Bulgaria decide to codify administrative penalty law, it is appropriate that the questions relating to the extinction of the administrative responsibility to be systemised into a separate section, which regulates the legal facts justifying the termination of proceedings for natural persons, sole traders and legal entities, as well as the statutory limitation periods for the liability of those entities. For this purpose, Bulgaria could consider the relevant comparative experience in this context (Box 4.23).

Box 4.23. Preclusive time periods and statutory limitations in Austria, Czech Republic, Germany, Lithuania, and the Netherlands

Austria

According to § 31 of the Austrian Act on Administrative offenses (Verwaltungsstrafgesetz):

"Section 31.

(1) The persecution of a person is inadmissible if no act of persecution (Section 32 (2)) has been carried out against them within a period of one year. This period is to be calculated from the point in time at which the criminal activity has been completed or the criminal behaviour has ceased; if the success related to the offense occurred later, the period does not run until this point in time.

(2) The criminal liability of an administrative offense expires by the statute of limitations. The limitation period is three years and begins at the point in time specified in Paragraph 1. The limitation period does not include:

1. the time during which, according to a legal regulation, the persecution cannot be initiated or continued;
2. the time during which criminal proceedings against the offender are being conducted with the public prosecutor, the court or another administrative authority;
3. the time during which the procedure is suspended until a final decision has been reached;
4. the time of proceedings before the Administrative Court, the Constitutional Court or the Court of Justice of the European Union.

(3) A sentence may no longer be carried out if three years have passed since it was finally imposed. The limitation period does not include:

1. the time of proceedings before the Administrative Court, the Constitutional Court or the Court of Justice of the European Union;
2. Times in which the execution of sentences was inadmissible, suspended, postponed or interrupted;
3. Times in which the offender was abroad."

Czech Republic

According to § 30 of the Act on administrative offenses of the Czech Republic the prescriptive period is one year for misdemeanours with a possible administrative penalty of less than CZK 100 000 (± EUR 3 930). For misdemeanours of at least CZK 100 000 this period is three years.

§ 31 and § 32 of this act provide for a detailed regulation of the setting and interruption of the prescriptive period. These provisions read as follows:

"§ 31 The running of the limitation period

(1) The limitation period shall begin to run on the day following the day on which the offense is committed; the day on which the offense is committed means the day on which the proceedings were concluded which the offense was committed. If the sign is a transfer to an effect, the limitation period shall begin to run on the day following that on which such effect occurs.

(2) The limitation period begins to run

(a) in the case of a continuing offense, on the following day after the day on which the last partial attack took place,

(b) in the case of a collective offense, on the day following the day on which the last attack took place, and

(c) in the case of a continuous offense, on the day following the day on which the unlawful removal took place condition.

(3) If the offender has committed more than one offense, he shall run for each of them the limitation period separately.

§ 32 Setting and interruption of the limitation period

(1) The limitation period does not include time,

(a) which has been the subject of a criminal offense for the same act management,

(b) after which the infringement proceedings have been suspended because a sentence could be expected to be imposed accused of a misdemeanour for another act in criminal proceedings, the administrative punishment that can be imposed in misdemeanour proceedings is insignificant in addition to punishment that could be imposed in a criminal offense management,

(c) after which the matter was the subject of administrative court proceedings,

(d) for which the conditional waiver of an administrative sentence has lasted.

(2) The limitation period is interrupted

(a) notification of the commencement of misdemeanour proceedings,

(b) by issuing a decision recognising the accused guilty,

(c) issuing a decision approving the settlement agreement; by interrupting the limitation period, the limitation period begins new.

(3) If the limitation period has been interrupted, the liability for the offense shall expire no later than 3 years from its commission; in the case of an offense for which the law sets the amount of the pecuniary sanction, the upper limit of which is at least CZK 100 000, liability for the offense expires no later than 5 years after its commission."

Germany

The German Act on Administrative Offenses (Ordnungswidrigkeitengesetz) has a rather detailed regulation of the setting and suspension of the prescription period. The relevant provisions read as follows:

"Section 31 Prosecution Barred by the Statute of Limitation

(1) Prosecution of regulatory offences and the ordering of incidental consequences shall be barred after the period of limitation has expired. Section 27 subsection 2 first sentence number 1 shall remain unaffected.

(2) If not otherwise provided by statute, the period of limitation for the prosecution of regulatory offences shall expire:

1. after three years in the case of regulatory offences for which a maximum regulatory pecuniary sanction of more than EUR 15 000 may be imposed,
2. after two years in the case of regulatory offences for which a maximum regulatory pecuniary sanction is imposable ranging from more than EUR 2 500 to EUR 15 000,

3. after one year in the case of regulatory offences for which a maximum regulatory pecuniary sanction is imposable ranging from more than EUR 1 000 to EUR 2 500,
4. after six months in all other cases involving regulatory offences.

(3) The statute of limitation shall begin to run as soon as the act is completed. If a result constituting a factual element of the offence occurs only later, the period of limitation shall begin to run at that time.

Section 32 Period of Limitation Tolled by Statute

(1) The period of limitation shall be tolled for as long as prosecution cannot be commenced or continued by operation of the statute. This shall not apply if the act cannot be prosecuted due to the absence of a request or authorisation.

(2) If prior to the expiry of the period of limitation a judgment of the court of first instance or a decision in accordance with section 72 has been rendered, the period of limitation shall not expire prior to the date on which the proceedings were concluded with final and binding effect.

Section 33 Period of Limitation Interrupted

(1) The period of limitation shall be interrupted by:

1. the initial examination of the person concerned, the notification that investigation proceedings have been initiated against him, or by the order requiring such examination or notification,
2. any judicial examination of the person concerned or of a witness, or by the order requiring such examination,
3. any appointment of an expert by the prosecuting authority or the judge, if the person concerned has previously been examined or was informed of the initiation of the investigation proceedings,
4. any order by the prosecuting authority or by the judge for seizure or search, and by judicial decisions by which such order is upheld,
5. the temporary discontinuation of the proceedings by the prosecuting authority or the judge because of absence of the person concerned, as well as by any order of the prosecuting authority or the judge issued after such discontinuation of the proceedings to establish the whereabouts of the person concerned or to secure evidence,
6. any request by the prosecuting authority or the judge to undertake an investigatory act in a foreign country,
7. the statutory hearing of another authority by the prosecuting authority prior to conclusion of the investigations,
8. the transfer of the case to the administrative authority by the public prosecution office in accordance with section 43,
9. issuance of a regulatory fining notice, so far as such notice is served within two weeks, otherwise by service thereof,
10. receipt of the files at the Local Court in accordance with section 69 subsection 3 first sentence and subsection 5 second sentence and referral of the case to the administrative authority in accordance with section 69 subsection 5 first sentence,
11. any fixing of a date for a main hearing,
12. reference to the possibility of giving a decision without a main hearing (section 72 subsection 1 second sentence),
13. preferring public charges,
14. the opening of main proceedings,
15. a penal order or any other decision equivalent to a judgment.

In independent proceedings involving an order imposing an incidental consequence or a regulatory pecuniary sanction against a legal person or an association of persons, the period of limitation shall be interrupted by the acts referred to in the first sentence for the purpose of carrying out independent proceedings.

(2) The running of the statute of limitations shall be interrupted by a written order or decision at the time at which the order or decision is signed. If the document has not immediately commenced processing after signing, then the time it is actually submitted for processing shall be decisive.

(3) After each interruption, the statute of limitations shall commence to run anew. However, prosecution shall be barred by the statute of limitations at the latest either when, since the time indicated in section 31 subsection 3 twice the statutory period of limitations has elapsed, or when at least two years have elapsed. If a person is charged with an act in proceedings pending at a court, which at the same time constitutes a criminal offence and a regulatory offence, then the period ensuing from the criminal penalty imposable shall be deemed to be the statutory period of limitations within the meaning of the second sentence. Section 32 shall remain unaffected.

(4) The interruption shall be effective only in respect of the person to whom the act relates. In cases falling under subsection 1 first sentence numbers 1 to 7, 11, and 13 to 15, the interruption shall also occur if the act is aimed at prosecution of the offence as a criminal offence.

Section 34 Execution Subject to the Statute of Limitations

(1) A regulatory pecuniary sanction imposed with final and binding effect may no longer be executed after expiry of the period of limitation.

(2) The period of limitation shall amount to

1. five years in the case of a regulatory pecuniary sanction exceeding EUR 1 000;
2. three years in the case of a regulatory pecuniary sanction not exceeding EUR 1 000.

(3) The period of limitation shall begin on the day on which the decision enters into final and binding effect.

(4) The statute of limitation shall be tolled for as long as:

1. execution may not be commenced or continued by operation of statute,
2. execution is suspended, or
3. easier means of payment have been granted.

(5) Subsections 1 to 4 shall apply mutatis mutandis to incidental consequences resulting in an obligation to pay. If such incidental consequences have been ordered in addition to a regulatory pecuniary sanction, execution of one legal consequence shall not fall under the statute of limitation earlier than that of the others."

Lithuania

Article 35 of the Code of administrative offenses of the Republic of Lithuania has detailed regulation of the prescriptive period of administrative penalties and the way this period is set and suspended. The provisions read as follows:

"Article 35. Time limits for imposing an administrative penalty

An administrative penalty may be imposed no later than six months from the date of the offense or, in the case of a continuous offense, within six months from the date on which it became apparent. An administrative penalty may be imposed for the infringements referred to in Section Twelve of this Code, as well as for the infringements provided for in Articles 413, 85, 1852, 1932, 20710, 20712, 209, 2091,

2092, 2093, 2094, 2095, 2096, 210, 21411 within six months from the date of the finding of the breach, if no more than one year has elapsed between the date of the breach and the date of its finding.

Refusing to initiate a pre-trial investigation into a criminal offense or imposing an economic sanction established by the laws of the Republic of Lithuania on an undertaking when the relevant administrative offense entails administrative liability, or terminating criminal proceedings or imposing an economic sanction on an undertaking the violation entails administrative liability, procedure, or after the acquittal of a court judgment, if the actions of the prosecuted person show signs of an administrative violation, an administrative penalty may be imposed no later than two months after the decision to refuse to initiate a pre-trial investigation or refuse to impose Lithuanian Economic sanction established in the laws of the Republic of Latvia for an economic entity when the liability, or from the decision to terminate the criminal proceedings or the imposition of an economic sanction established in the laws of the Republic of Lithuania on the economic entity, when the relevant administrative offense entails administrative liability, the procedure, or from the effective date of the acquittal.

If the person subject to administrative responsibility does not have a permanent residence, is away or lives abroad for a long time, is ill, has been searched or if the issue of administrative liability cannot be resolved due to an investigation or other reasons, the time limits referred to in paragraphs 1 and 2 shall be extended. whether or not an administrative offense report has been drawn up for the person to be prosecuted, but not for more than one year, counting from the date of the offense or its discovery or from the decision to refuse to open a pre-trial investigation or to terminate criminal proceedings, whether to impose an economic sanction established in the laws of the Republic of Lithuania on an economic entity when the relevant administrative violation of law entails administrative liability for the person, or to terminate the sanctioning procedure, or from the acquittal court date of adoption.

In the cases provided for in the second and third paragraphs of this Article, no administrative penalty may be imposed if more than two years have elapsed since the date of the administrative offense.

When the decision to impose an economic sanction established in the laws of the Republic of Lithuania on an economic entity, when the relevant administrative offense is committed, renders the person administratively liable, or terminates the sanctioning procedure or the date on which the decision of the appellate court takes effect."

The Netherlands

According to the regulation of administrative pecuniary sanctions in the General Administrative Law act the prescriptive period of the power to impose administrative penalties is five years after the transgression was committed. Only in the few cases involving lighter transgressions this period is three years. The term of three years is the same prescriptive period as the one that applies in criminal law for offences, which is the lighter category for criminal offenses (see article 70 DCC). According to the third paragraph of this provision the prescription period will be suspended during objection or appeal.

The relevant provision, which applies to administrative penalties provided in all legislation, is the following:

"Article 5:45

(1) If article 5:53 applies, the power to impose an administrative pecuniary sanction expires five years after the violation took place.

(2) In all other cases the power to impose an administrative pecuniary sanction expires three years after the violation took place.

(3) If an objection or appeal is lodged against an administrative pecuniary sanction, the expiry period is suspended until a final decision is given on the objection or appeal."

Source: OECD Research.

4.15. The AVPA could introduce the possibility to delete the administrative penalty from the record some time after its application

Under the current regulation of administrative liability, there is no institution similar to the rehabilitation of protected persons under Article 86 and the following articles of the Penal Code. In other words, the fact that an administrative penalty has been imposed is not deleted from the record even after its application.

It is noteworthy that such a mechanism is provided for those who have committed a crime, but not for those who have committed administrative violations. This legal gap also impacts the legal status of the persons who have committed a crime and have been released from criminal liability by having an administrative penalty.

A possible solution would be to create a new Article 82b with the wording as proposed in Box 4.24, which would be in line with the practice in other EU countries like Slovenia (Box 4.25).

Box 4.24. Proposed Article 82(a)

"Article 82a.

(1) The person on whom an administrative penalty has been imposed shall not be deemed to be punished after the expiry of:

1. two years after the sentence has been served;
2. two years after the expiry of the period referred to in Article 82 (3), where the penalty imposed has not been executed and, where the administrative penalty imposed is a pecuniary sanction, for the recovery of which enforcement proceedings have been initiated, two years after the expiry of the time limits laid down in Article 171 of the Tax Code — the Insurance Procedure Code.

(2) Where the person is punished for two or more infringements, the time limit referred to in paragraph 1 shall run for each of them separately.

(3) The provisions referred to in paragraphs (1) and (2) shall also apply respectively to sole traders and legal persons on whom a financial penalty has been imposed."

Note: A text with a similar wording has been discussed by the working group for the preparation of Amendment Law of AVPA, adopted by the National Assembly at the end of 2020, promulgated, SG, no. 109 of 2020, but did not become part of the final bill submitted to the National Assembly. Paragraphs 2 and 3 are proposed by the OECD based on the discussion in the working group.

Box 4.25. Deletion of minor offence decisions, judgments and orders in Slovenia

"Article 205

Final minor offence decisions, judgments and orders shall be deleted from the records referred to in Articles 203 and 204 of this Act upon the expiry of a three-year period from the day they became final, but not until secondary sanctions cease to have effect; the documentary materials on the basis of which they were entered shall be kept in accordance with the provision of paragraph seven of Article 206 of this Act."

Source: Minor Offences Act – ZP-1 (Official Gazette of the Republic of Slovenia [Uradni list RS], No. 7/03 of 23 January 2003).

References

European Committee on Crime Problems (2020), *Replies to Questionnaire on Administrative Sanctions*, https://rm.coe.int/cdpc-2019-1-replies-to-questionnaire-on-administrative-sanctions/168093669b (accessed on 24 June 2021). [2]

OECD (2021), *Implementing the OECD Anti-Bribery Convention. Phase 4 Report: Bulgaria*, OECD, Paris, https://www.oecd.org/corruption/bulgaria-oecdanti-briberyconvention.htm (accessed on 27 October 2021). [1]

www.ingramcontent.com/pod-product-compliance
Lightning Source LLC
LaVergne TN
LVHW081410110826
845149LV00010B/1690